easy
christmas

D1335884

easy christmas

100 fuss-free recipes for festive cooking

M&S

Marks and Spencer p.l.c.
PO Box 3339
Chester CH99 9QS

shop online

www.marksandspencer.com

Copyright © Exclusive Editions Publishing Ltd 2011

All rights reserved. No part of this publication may be reproduced,
stored in a retrieval system or transmitted, in any form or by any
means, electronic, mechanical, photocopying, recording or
otherwise, without the prior permission of the copyright holder.

ISBN: 978-1-84960-755-1

Printed in China

Introduction by Linda Doeser
New recipes by Teresa Goldfinch
Cover and additional photography by Clive Streeter
Cover and additional food styling by Teresa Goldfinch

The views expressed in this book are those of the author but they
are general views only and readers are urged to consult a relevant
and qualified specialist for individual advice in particular situations.
Marks and Spencer p.l.c. and Exclusive Editions Limited hereby
exclude all liability to the extent permitted by law for any errors
or omissions in this book and for any loss, damage or expense
(whether direct or indirect) suffered by a third party relying on any
information contained in this book.

Notes for the Reader
This book uses both metric and imperial measurements. Follow
the same units of measurement throughout; do not mix metric and
imperial. All spoon measurements are level: teaspoons are assumed
to be 5 ml, and tablespoons are assumed to be 15 ml. Unless
otherwise stated, milk is assumed to be full fat, eggs and individual
vegetables are medium, and pepper is freshly ground black pepper.

The times given are an approximate guide only. Preparation times
differ according to the techniques used by different people and
the cooking times may also vary from those given. Optional
ingredients, variations or serving suggestions have not been
included in the calculations.

Recipes using raw or very lightly cooked eggs should be avoided
by infants, the elderly, pregnant women, convalescents and anyone
suffering from an illness. Pregnant and breastfeeding women are
advised to avoid eating peanuts and peanut products. Sufferers
from nut allergies should be aware that some of the ready-made
ingredients used in the recipes in this book may contain nuts.
Always check the packaging before use.

For front cover recipe see p.170.

Contents

Introduction

Scrumptious meals, edible treats, tasty snacks and delicious drinks are an essential part of Christmas celebrations. It's a time of year when family, friends and neighbours get together to enjoy each other's company and the good things in life, but it can be hard work and cause a great deal of stress for the family cook. However, it doesn't have to be endless toil and non-stop slaving over a hot stove – everyone should have fun and some time off.

Christmas dinner is invariably the main event but the festive period traditionally extends over 12 days, and that doesn't even include Christmas Eve. While you may not be entertaining guests the whole time, neighbours pop round, kids' friends visit and people you haven't seen for ages decide to renew old acquaintances. These days family members tend to live further apart than they did in the past, so you may also have house guests for a few days and, of course, there's New Year's Eve to celebrate.

It will inevitably require extra effort if you are entertaining over Christmas, but with careful planning, some cooking in advance, easy-to-follow recipes and a bit of cheating, you can still dazzle your guests with a sparkling array of festive fare and have time to enjoy their company. Every January, we promise ourselves that we'll start buying presents and organizing the festivities for next Christmas in October or even earlier, and every year we tend to leave it to the last minute when the queues are long, the weather is horrible and the must-have presents have disappeared from the shelves. Then you don't find out until late on Christmas Eve that your cousin has become a vegan and your teenager has invited her boyfriend to Boxing Day lunch.

Plan your guest list, whether for Christmas dinner or a drinks party, well in advance, highlighting anyone who has special dietary needs. Then start writing more lists – it's boring but will make life far less stressful in the long run. Browse through the recipes here, making a separate list for each special occasion and adding any necessary extras, such as fresh salads for the buffet table and olives and nuts to accompany pre-dinner drinks. Pin these up in the kitchen, allowing yourself enough time to change your mind, cross some things off and add others. Then, when it's time to buy and prepare everything, you will know exactly what you are doing.

Top Tips for Success

• Make a countdown list of things that can be prepared in advance and frozen, things that can be prepared a day or two ahead and stored in the refrigerator or in airtight containers and things that must be done on the day. This will be invaluable when you're writing shopping lists, making it less likely that anything will be overlooked.

• Make a note on the kitchen calendar or write yet another list of what needs to be taken out of the freezer for thawing and when.

• Make a precise timetable for preparing Christmas dinner and any other special meals that includes every last detail from preheating the oven to opening the red wine. Pin it up in the kitchen.

• Check stocks of everyday, non-festive items such as breakfast cereals, pet food and washing-up liquid that are easily overlooked when you're preoccupied with planning a special occasion and have guests staying.

• Make a note on the kitchen calendar of anything, such as a goose or whole salmon, that you need to order in advance and a note of when it is to be collected or delivered.

• Take advantage of local supermarket deliveries and order heavy and non-perishable items, such as wine, soft drinks, mixers, frozen pastry, coffee, pickles and sugar. Do this well in advance as the delivery slots fill up quickly at this time of year.

• Make use of the family – you don't have to do every last thing yourself. Give them specific jobs, such as checking that the salt mill and pepper grinder are full, peeling vegetables, laying or clearing the table and stacking the dishwasher, depending on their ages. Agree this with them in advance, write a list and pin it up in the kitchen.

• Accept sensible offers of help from guests, especially anyone who is staying with you. Washing up the special wine glasses or making a pot of tea is one way that they can thank you for your hospitality.

• Give yourself a break and bear in mind that you're not running a hotel or restaurant. Your guests want to spend time with you and enjoy your company. Also, you'll make them feel uncomfortable if there's an endless procession of cakes, biscuits, nibbles, snacks and other goodies that can become too much of a good thing. Be organised but remember to relax and enjoy yourself!

Appetizers & Party Nibbles

wild mushroom & sherry soup

SERVES 4

2 tbsp olive oil

1 onion, chopped

1 garlic clove, chopped

125 g/4½ oz sweet potato, chopped

1 leek, sliced

200 g/7 oz button and chestnut mushrooms

150 g/5½ oz mixed wild mushrooms

600 ml/1 pint vegetable stock

350 ml/12 fl oz single cream

4 tbsp dry sherry

salt and pepper

Parmesan cheese shavings and sautéed wild mushrooms, to garnish

1 Heat the oil in a saucepan over a medium heat. Add the onion and garlic and cook, stirring, for 3 minutes, until slightly softened. Add the sweet potato and cook, stirring, for 3 minutes. Add the leek and cook, stirring, for 2 minutes.

2 Stir in the mushrooms, stock and cream. Bring to the boil, then reduce the heat and simmer gently, stirring occasionally, for 25 minutes. Remove from the heat, stir in the sherry and leave to cool slightly.

3 Transfer half the soup to a food processor and blend until smooth. Return the mixture to the saucepan with the rest of the soup, season to taste with salt and pepper and reheat gently, stirring. Pour into 4 warmed soup bowls and garnish with Parmesan cheese shavings and sautéed wild mushrooms. Serve immediately.

creamy carrot & parsnip soup

SERVES 4

55 g/2 oz butter

1 large onion, chopped

450 g/1 lb carrots, chopped

2 large parsnips, chopped

1 tbsp grated fresh ginger

1 tsp grated orange rind

600 ml/1 pint vegetable stock

125 ml/4 fl oz single cream

salt and pepper

sprigs of fresh coriander, to garnish

1 Melt the butter in a large saucepan over a low heat. Add the onion and cook, stirring, for 3 minutes, until slightly softened. Add the carrots and parsnips, cover the pan and cook, stirring occasionally, for about 15 minutes, until the vegetables have softened a little. Stir in the ginger, orange rind and stock. Bring to the boil, then reduce the heat, cover the pan and simmer for 30–35 minutes, until the vegetables are tender. Remove from the heat and leave to cool for 10 minutes.

2 Transfer the soup to a food processor and blend until smooth. Return the soup to the rinsed-out saucepan, stir in the cream and season well with salt and pepper. Warm through gently over a low heat.

3 Remove from the heat and ladle into 4 warmed soup bowls. Garnish each bowl with pepper and a sprig of coriander and serve immediately.

spiced pumpkin soup

SERVES 4

2 tbsp olive oil

1 onion, chopped

1 garlic clove, chopped

1 tbsp chopped fresh ginger

1 small red chilli, deseeded and finely chopped

2 tbsp chopped fresh coriander

1 bay leaf

1 kg/2 lb 4 oz pumpkin, peeled, deseeded and diced

600 ml/1 pint vegetable stock

salt and pepper

single cream, to garnish

1 Heat the oil in a saucepan over a medium heat. Add the onion and garlic and cook, stirring, for 4 minutes, until slightly softened. Add the ginger, chilli, coriander, bay leaf and pumpkin and cook, stirring, for 3 minutes.

2 Pour in the stock and bring to the boil. Using a slotted spoon, skim any foam from the surface. Reduce the heat and simmer gently, stirring occasionally, for 25 minutes, or until the pumpkin is tender. Remove from the heat, take out and discard the bay leaf and leave to cool slightly.

3 Transfer the soup to a food processor and blend until smooth. Return the mixture to the saucepan and season to taste with salt and pepper. Reheat gently, stirring. Remove from the heat, pour into 4 warmed soup bowls, garnish each one with a swirl of cream and serve immediately.

filo-wrapped asparagus with parmesan

SERVES 6

**18 plump asparagus
spears, tough ends
snapped off**

**3 sheets filo pastry,
each measuring about
45 x 24 cm/17¾ x 9½
inches**

**125 g/4½ oz butter, melted,
plus extra for greasing**

**90 g/3¼ oz freshly grated
Parmesan cheese**

salt

dip

**150 ml/5 fl oz good-quality
mayonnaise**

**150 ml/5 fl oz natural
yogurt**

**10–12 fresh basil leaves,
torn into small pieces**

**1 garlic clove, peeled and
crushed (optional)**

1 Blanch the asparagus in a saucepan of lightly salted boiling water for 30–40 seconds, then transfer to a bowl of cold water using a slotted spoon. Drain and pat dry with kitchen paper.

2 Preheat the oven to 200°C/400°F/Gas Mark 6. Lay one sheet of the filo pastry on a work surface, covering the remaining sheets with a damp tea towel to prevent them from drying out. Brush the sheet of filo with a little of the melted butter and sprinkle with one third of the Parmesan, then cut into six rectangles, each measuring about 15 x 12 cm/6 x 4½ inches

3 Place an asparagus spear at one end of each rectangle and roll up. Transfer to a lightly greased baking tray. Repeat with the remaining pastry, Parmesan and asparagus. Brush with the remaining butter and bake in the preheated oven for 12–14 minutes, until crisp and golden brown.

4 To make the dip, mix together the mayonnaise, yogurt, basil and garlic, if using, in a small bowl. Serve the filo-wrapped asparagus warm or cold with the dip.

festive prawn cocktail

SERVES 8

125 ml/4 fl oz tomato ketchup

1 tsp chilli sauce

1 tsp Worcestershire sauce

2 ruby grapefruits

1 kg/2 lb 4 oz cooked tiger prawns, peeled and deveined

lettuce leaves, shredded

2 avocados, peeled, stoned and diced

lime slices and fresh dill sprigs, to garnish

mayonnaise

2 large egg yolks

1 tsp English mustard powder

1 tsp salt

300 ml/10 fl oz groundnut oil

1 tsp white wine vinegar

pepper

1 First make the mayonnaise. Put the egg yolks in a bowl, add the mustard powder, pepper to taste and salt and beat together well. Pour the oil into a jug and make sure that your bowl is secure on the work surface by sitting it on a damp cloth. Using an electric or hand whisk, begin to whisk the egg yolks, adding just one drop of the oil. Make sure that this has been thoroughly absorbed before adding another drop and whisking well.

2 Continue adding the oil one drop at a time until the mixture thickens and stiffens – at this point, whisk in the vinegar and then continue to dribble in the remaining oil very slowly in a thin stream, whisking constantly, until you have used up all the oil and you have a thick mayonnaise.

3 Mix the mayonnaise, tomato ketchup, chilli sauce and Worcestershire sauce together in a small bowl. Cover with clingfilm and refrigerate until required.

4 Cut off a slice from the top and bottom of each grapefruit, then peel off the skin and all the white pith. Cut between the membranes to separate the segments.

5 When ready to serve, make a bed of shredded lettuce in the bases of 8 glass dishes. Divide the prawns, grapefruit segments and avocados between them and spoon over the mayonnaise dressing. Serve the cocktails garnished with lime slices and dill sprigs.

chicken liver pâté

SERVES 4–6

200 g/7 oz butter

225 g/8 oz trimmed chicken livers, thawed if frozen

2 tbsp Marsala or brandy

1½ tsp chopped fresh sage

1 garlic clove, roughly chopped

150 ml/5 fl oz double cream

salt and pepper

fresh bay leaves or sage leaves, to garnish

Melba toast, to serve

1 Melt 40 g/1½ oz of the butter in a large, heavy-based frying pan. Add the chicken livers and cook over a medium heat for 4 minutes on each side. They should be browned on the outside but still pink in the centre. Transfer to a food processor and process until finely chopped.

2 Add the Marsala to the frying pan and stir, scraping up any sediment with a wooden spoon, then add to the food processor with the chopped sage, garlic and 100 g/3½ oz of the remaining butter. Process until smooth. Add the cream, season to taste with salt and pepper and process until thoroughly combined and smooth. Spoon the pâté into a dish or individual ramekins, smooth the surface and leave to cool completely.

3 Melt the remaining butter in a small saucepan, then spoon it over the surface of the pâté, leaving any sediment in the saucepan. Decorate with herb leaves, leave to cool, then cover and chill in the refrigerator. Serve with Melba toast.

smoked turkey & stuffing parcels

MAKES 12

12 slices smoked turkey breast

4 tbsp cranberry sauce or jelly

400 g/14 oz cooked and cooled sausage-meat stuffing

24 sheets filo pastry

70 g/2½ oz butter, melted

1 Preheat the oven to 190°C/375°F/Gas Mark 5. Put a non-stick baking sheet into the oven to heat.

2 For each parcel, spread a slice of smoked turkey with a teaspoonful of cranberry sauce, spoon 35 g/1¼ oz of the stuffing into the centre and roll up the turkey slice. Lay one sheet of filo pastry on a work surface and brush with a little of the melted butter. Put another sheet on top, then put the rolled-up turkey in the centre. Add a little more cranberry sauce, then carefully fold the filo pastry around the turkey, tucking under the ends to form a neat parcel. Repeat to make 12 parcels.

3 Place the parcels on the hot baking sheet, brush with the remaining melted butter and bake in the preheated oven for 25 minutes until golden. Serve hot.

devils & angels on horseback

MAKES 32

devils

8 rindless lean bacon rashers

8 canned anchovy fillets in oil, drained

16 whole blanched almonds

16 ready-to-eat prunes

angels

8 rindless lean bacon rashers

16 smoked oysters, drained if canned

sprigs of fresh thyme, to garnish

1 Preheat the oven to 200°C/400°F/Gas Mark 6. For the devils, cut each bacon rasher lengthways in half and gently stretch with the back of a knife. Cut each anchovy fillet lengthways in half. Wrap half an anchovy around each almond and press them into the cavity where the stones have been removed from the prunes. Wrap a strip of bacon around each prune and secure with a cocktail stick.

2 For the angels, cut each bacon rasher lengthways in half and gently stretch with the back of a knife. Wrap a bacon strip around each oyster and secure with a cocktail stick.

3 Put the devils and angels onto a baking sheet and cook in the preheated oven for 10–15 minutes until sizzling hot and the bacon is cooked. Garnish with sprigs of fresh thyme and serve hot.

mixed antipasto meat platter

SERVES 4

1 cantaloupe melon

55 g/2 oz Italian salami, sliced thinly

8 slices prosciutto

8 slices bresaola

8 slices mortadella

4 plum tomatoes, sliced thinly

4 fresh figs, halved

115 g/4 oz black olives, stoned

2 tbsp shredded fresh basil leaves

4 tbsp extra virgin olive oil, plus extra for serving

pepper

1 Cut the melon in half, scoop out and discard the seeds, then cut the flesh into 8 wedges. Arrange the wedges on one half of a large serving platter.

2 Arrange the salami, prosciutto, bresaola and mortadella in loose folds on the other half of the platter. Arrange the tomato slices and fig halves on the platter.

3 Scatter the olives over the antipasto. Sprinkle the basil over the tomatoes and drizzle with olive oil. Season to taste with pepper, then serve with extra olive oil.

beef carpaccio

SERVES 6

**500 g/1 lb 2 oz beef fillet,
cut from the thin end of
the fillet**

**200 ml/7 fl oz extra virgin
olive oil**

50 g/1¾ oz pine kernels

200 g/7 oz rocket

25 g/1 oz Parmesan cheese

2 tsp truffle oil

salt and pepper

1 Put the beef in the freezer for an hour before use, to firm it up for easier cutting. Trim any fat or sinew from the beef, then cut the fillet into slices as thin as you can manage.

2 Lay a slice of beef on a chopping board and, using a flat, broad knife, press against the meat, pushing down hard and pulling towards yourself in a spreading motion several times across each slice, trying not to tear it too much. As well as making the fillet thin, this will tenderize it. Repeat with all the beef slices.

3 Pour a little pool of olive oil into a wide dish. Place a layer of beef on the oil, season lightly with salt and pepper and pour over some more olive oil. Repeat until all the beef has been seasoned in this way. Cover the dish with clingfilm and refrigerate for 30 minutes to 2 hours. Heat the pine kernels in a dry frying pan over a medium heat, until lightly toasted, and set aside.

4 When you're ready to eat, lay a bed of rocket on 6 serving plates, then remove the beef slices from the marinade and divide evenly between the plates. Scatter with the pine kernels and shave the Parmesan cheese over, using a vegetable peeler. Lay a few extra leaves of rocket on top of each plate and drizzle over a few drops of truffle oil to serve.

scallops wrapped in pancetta

MAKES 12

12 fresh rosemary sprigs

6 raw scallops, corals removed

12 thin-cut pancetta rashers

dressing

2 tbsp olive oil

1 tbsp white wine vinegar

1 tsp honey

salt and pepper

1 First prepare the rosemary by stripping most of the leaves off the stalks, leaving a cluster of leaves at the top. Trim the stalks to about 6 cm/2½ inches long, cutting each sprig at an angle at the base.

2 Cut each scallop in half through the centre to give 2 discs of scallop, wrap each one in a pancetta rasher and, keeping the end tucked under, place on a plate. Cover and chill in the refrigerator for 15 minutes.

3 To make the dressing, whisk the oil, vinegar and honey together in a small bowl and season to taste with salt and pepper.

4 Preheat the grill to high or heat a ridged griddle pan over a high heat. Cook the scallops under the grill or on the griddle pan for 2 minutes on each side until the pancetta is crisp and brown. Spear each one on a prepared rosemary skewer and serve hot, with the dressing as a dip.

turkey club sandwiches

SERVES 6

**12 pancetta or streaky
bacon rashers**

18 slices white bread

**1 quantity mayonnaise
(see page 18)**

**12 slices cooked turkey
breast meat**

3 tomatoes, sliced

6 Little Gem lettuce leaves

6 stuffed olives

salt and pepper

1 Grill or fry the pancetta until crisp, drain on kitchen
paper and keep warm. Toast the bread until golden, then
cut off the crusts.

2 You will need 3 slices of toast for each sandwich. For
each sandwich, spread the first piece of toast with a
generous amount of mayonnaise, top with 2 slices of turkey,
keeping the edges neat, and then top with a couple of slices
of tomato. Season to taste with salt and pepper.

3 Add another slice of toast and top with 2 pancetta
rashers and 1 lettuce leaf. Season to taste again with
salt and pepper, add a little more mayonnaise, then top with
the final piece of toast. Push a cocktail stick or a decorative
sparkler through a stuffed olive, and then push this through
the sandwich to hold it together.

devilled turkey legs

SERVES 4

2 turkey legs, skinned

½ tsp cayenne pepper

2 tbsp Dijon or hot mustard

40 g/1½ oz unsalted butter, softened

salt and pepper

sprigs of fresh flat leaf parsley, to garnish

1 Make deep criss-cross slashes in the turkey legs. Season with salt and pepper and sprinkle with a little of the cayenne pepper. Spread the mustard all over the legs, pressing it well into the slashes. Place the legs in a large, deep dish, cover with clingfilm and leave to marinate in the refrigerator for 6–8 hours.

2 Meanwhile, cream the butter in a bowl, then beat in the remaining cayenne pepper to taste. Cover the bowl with clingfilm and leave until you are ready to serve.

3 Preheat the grill. Place the turkey legs on a grill rack and cook under the grill, turning frequently, for 15–20 minutes, or until golden brown and cooked through. Test by inserting the point of a sharp knife in the thickest part. If the juices run clear, the turkey is cooked.

4 Transfer the turkey legs to a carving board and carve into slices. Arrange in a serving dish, garnished with parsley. Serve immediately with the cayenne butter.

mozzarella crostini with pesto & caviar

SERVES 4

**8 slices white bread,
crusts removed**

3 tbsp olive oil

**200 g/7 oz firm mozzarella
cheese, diced**

6 tbsp lumpfish roe

pesto

**75 g/2¾ oz fresh basil,
finely chopped**

**35 g/1¼ oz pine kernels,
finely chopped**

**2 garlic cloves, finely
chopped**

3 tbsp olive oil

1 Preheat the oven to 180°C/350°F/Gas Mark 4. Using a sharp knife, cut the bread into fancy shapes, such as half-moons, stars and Christmas trees. Drizzle with the oil, transfer to an ovenproof dish and bake in the preheated oven for 15 minutes.

2 While the bread is baking, make the pesto. Put the basil, pine kernels and garlic in a small bowl. Pour in the oil and stir well.

3 Remove the bread shapes from the oven and leave to cool. Spread a layer of pesto on the shapes, top each one with a piece of mozzarella and some lumpfish roe and serve.

cheese straws

MAKES 24

**115 g/4 oz plain flour,
plus extra for dusting**

pinch of salt

1 tsp curry powder

**55 g/2 oz butter, plus extra
for greasing**

**55 g/2 oz grated Cheddar
cheese**

1 egg, beaten

**poppy and cumin seeds,
for sprinkling**

1 Sift the flour, salt and curry powder into a bowl. Add the butter and rub in until the mixture resembles breadcrumbs. Add the cheese and half the egg and mix to form a dough. Wrap in clingfilm and chill in the refrigerator for 30 minutes.

2 Preheat the oven to 200°C/400°F/Gas Mark 6, then grease several baking trays. On a floured work surface, roll out the dough to 5 mm/¼ inch thick. Cut into 7.5 x 1-cm/3 x ½-inch strips. Pinch the strips lightly along the sides and place on the prepared baking trays.

3 Brush the strips with the remaining egg and sprinkle half with poppy seeds and half with cumin seeds. Bake in the preheated oven for 10–15 minutes, or until golden. Transfer to wire racks to cool.

honey sesame sausages

MAKES 24

2 tbsp clear honey

1 tbsp olive oil, plus extra for oiling

24 lean cocktail pork sausages

2 tbsp sesame seeds

1 Preheat the oven to 190°C/375°F/Gas Mark 5. Brush a non-stick baking sheet with a little oil and place in the oven.

2 Whisk the honey and oil together in a large bowl, add the sausages and toss well to coat.

3 Spread the sesame seeds out on a large piece of greaseproof paper and roll each sausage in the seeds until well coated.

4 Remove the baking sheet from the oven and place the sausages on it. Bake the sausages in the preheated oven for 10 minutes. Turn the sausages over and bake for a further 10–15 minutes until well browned and sticky.

5 Serve warm or cold, either with cocktail sticks or in individual bowls.

double cheese soufflés

MAKES 6

**25 g/1 oz butter, plus extra
for greasing**

**2 tbsp finely grated
Parmesan cheese**

175 ml/6 fl oz milk

25 g/1 oz self-raising flour

whole nutmeg, for grating

**100 g/3½ oz soft goat's
cheese**

**70 g/2½ oz mature Cheddar
cheese, grated**

2 large eggs, separated

salt and pepper

1 Preheat the oven to 200°C/400°F/Gas Mark 6. Put a baking sheet in the oven to warm. Generously grease the inside of 6 small ramekins with butter, add half the Parmesan cheese and shake to coat the butter.

2 Warm the milk in a small saucepan. Melt the remaining butter in a separate saucepan over a medium heat. Add the flour to the butter, stir well to combine and cook, stirring, for 2 minutes until smooth. Add a little of the warmed milk and stir until absorbed. Continue to add the milk a little at a time, stirring constantly, until you have a rich, smooth sauce. Season to taste with salt and pepper, and grate in a little nutmeg. Add the goat's and Cheddar cheeses to the sauce and stir until well combined and melted.

3 Remove from the heat and leave the sauce to cool a little, then add the egg yolks and stir to combine. In a separate bowl, whisk the egg whites until stiff. Fold a tablespoonful of the egg whites into the cheese sauce, then gradually fold in the remaining egg whites. Spoon into the prepared ramekins and scatter over the remaining Parmesan cheese.

4 Place the ramekins on the hot baking sheet and bake in the preheated oven for 15 minutes until puffed up and brown. Remove from the oven and serve immediately. The soufflés will collapse quite quickly when taken from the oven, so have your serving plates ready to take the soufflés to the table.

chestnut, madeira & mushroom tarts

MAKES 12

pastry

**225 g/8 oz plain flour,
plus extra for dusting**

pinch of salt

**100 g/3½ oz unsalted
butter, chilled and diced,
plus extra for greasing**

filling

25 g/1 oz unsalted butter

1 tsp olive oil

1 shallot, finely chopped

1 garlic clove, crushed

**8 cooked chestnuts, peeled
and roughly chopped**

**200 g/7 oz chestnut
mushrooms, chopped**

2 tbsp Madeira

**150 ml/5 fl oz double
cream**

1 egg, plus 1 egg yolk

salt and pepper

**chopped fresh parsley,
to serve**

1 Lightly grease a 7.5-cm/3-inch, 12-hole muffin tin with butter. Sift the flour into a large bowl, add the salt and rub in the remaining butter until the mixture resembles breadcrumbs. Add just enough cold water to bring the dough together. Knead briefly on a floured work surface.

2 Divide the pastry in half. Roll out one piece of pastry and, using a 9-cm/3½-inch plain pastry cutter, cut out 6 rounds, then roll each one into a 12-cm/4½-inch round. Repeat with the remaining pastry until you have 12 rounds of pastry, then use to line the muffin tin. Chill for 30 minutes.

3 Preheat the oven to 200°C/400°F/Gas Mark 6. To make the filling, melt the butter with the oil in a small frying pan over a low heat. Add the shallot and garlic and cook, stirring occasionally, for 5–8 minutes until the shallot is transparent and soft. Add the chestnuts and mushrooms and cook, stirring, for 2 minutes, then add the Madeira and simmer for 2 minutes.

4 Line the pastry cases with baking paper and fill with baking beans, then bake in the preheated oven for 10 minutes. Carefully lift out the paper and beans, and reduce the oven temperature to 190°C/375°F/Gas Mark 5. Stir the cream, whole egg and egg yolk into the mushroom mixture and season well with salt and pepper. Divide between the pastry cases and bake for 10 minutes. Leave to cool in the tin for 5 minutes, then carefully remove from the tin, scatter with chopped parsley and serve.

leek & bacon tartlets

MAKES 12

pastry

**225 g/8 oz plain flour,
plus extra for dusting**

pinch of salt

½ tsp paprika

**100 g/3½ oz unsalted
butter, chilled and diced,
plus extra for greasing**

filling

25 g/1 oz unsalted butter

1 tsp olive oil

1 leek, chopped

**8 unsmoked streaky bacon
rashers, cut into lardons**

2 eggs, beaten

**150 ml/5 fl oz double
cream**

1 tsp snipped fresh chives

salt and pepper

1 Lightly grease a 7.5-cm/3-inch, 12-hole muffin tin with butter. Sift the flour, salt and paprika into a bowl and rub in the remaining butter until the mixture resembles breadcrumbs. Add just enough cold water to bring the dough together. Knead briefly on a floured work surface.

2 Divide the pastry in half. Roll out one piece of pastry and, using a 9-cm/3½-inch plain cutter, cut out 6 rounds, then roll each one into a 12-cm/4½-inch round. Repeat with the other half of the pastry until you have 12 rounds, then use to line the muffin tin. Chill for 30 minutes.

3 Preheat the oven to 200°C/400°F/Gas Mark 6. To make the filling, melt the butter with the oil in a non-stick frying pan over a medium heat, add the leek and cook, stirring frequently, for 5 minutes until soft. Remove with a slotted spoon and set aside. Add the lardons to the frying pan and cook for 5 minutes, or until crisp. Drain on kitchen paper.

4 Line the pastry cases with baking paper and baking beans and bake in the preheated oven for 10 minutes. Whisk the eggs and cream together in a bowl, season to taste with salt and pepper, then stir in the chives with the cooked leek and bacon. Remove the pastry cases from the oven and carefully lift out the paper and beans. Divide the bacon and leek mixture between the pastry cases and bake for 10 minutes until the tarts are golden and risen. Leave to cool in the tin for 5 minutes, then carefully transfer to a wire rack. Serve warm or cold.

gravadlax

SERVES 8–12

**2 salmon fillets, with skin
on, about 450 g/1 lb each**

**6 tbsp roughly chopped
fresh dill**

115 g/4 oz sea salt

50 g/1¾ oz sugar

**1 tbsp roughly crushed
white peppercorns**

**12 slices brown bread,
buttered, to serve**

to garnish
lemon wedges
fresh dill sprigs

1 Rinse the salmon fillets under cold running water and dry with kitchen paper. Put one fillet, skin-side down, in a non-metallic dish.

2 Mix the dill, sea salt, sugar and peppercorns together in a small bowl. Spread this mixture over the fillet in the dish and put the second fillet, skin-side up, on top. Put a plate, the same size as the fish, on top and weigh down with 3–4 food cans.

3 Chill in the refrigerator for 2 days, turning the fish about every 12 hours and basting with any juices that come out of the fish.

4 Remove the salmon from the brine and thinly slice, without slicing the skin, as you would smoked salmon. Cut the buttered bread into triangles and serve with the salmon. Garnish with lemon wedges and dill sprigs.

corn & parmesan fritters

MAKES 25–30

**5 fresh corn cobs or 500 g/
1 lb 2 oz frozen or canned
sweetcorn kernels**

2 eggs, beaten

4 tbsp plain flour

**2 tbsp finely grated
Parmesan cheese**

1 tsp bicarbonate of soda

4 tbsp milk

vegetable oil, for frying

salt

1 If you are using fresh corn cobs, cook them in a large saucepan of boiling water for 7 minutes, then drain well. Stand them on their ends, cut away the kernels and leave to cool. If using frozen sweetcorn kernels, leave to thaw first, or drain canned sweetcorn kernels.

2 Put the sweetcorn kernels in a bowl with the eggs, flour, Parmesan cheese, bicarbonate of soda and a pinch of salt. Mix together, then add the milk and stir together well.

3 Heat the oil to a depth of 4 cm/1½ inches in a deep saucepan to a temperature of 180°C/350°F, or until a cube of bread browns in 30 seconds. Drop 4 teaspoonfuls of the mixture into the oil at a time and cook for 2 minutes. Turn over and cook for a further minute or so, or until crisp, brown and slightly puffed up. Remove and drain on kitchen paper. Keep warm while you cook the remaining batches of mixture – you may need to add a little more oil between batches and scoop out any stray sweetcorn kernels. Sprinkle with salt to serve.

figs with blue cheese

SERVES 6

12 ripe figs

350 g/12 oz Spanish blue cheese, such as Picós, crumbled

extra virgin olive oil, for drizzling

caramelized almonds

100 g/3½ oz caster sugar

115 g/4 oz blanched whole almonds

butter, for greasing

1 First make the caramelized almonds. Place the sugar in a saucepan over a medium heat and stir until the sugar melts and turns golden brown and bubbles. Do not stir once the mixture begins to bubble. Remove the saucepan from the heat, add the almonds one at a time and quickly turn with a fork until coated. Transfer each almond to a lightly greased baking sheet once it is coated. Leave until cool and firm. If the caramel hardens, return the saucepan to the heat.

2 To serve, slice the figs in half and arrange 4 halves on individual serving plates. Roughly chop the almonds by hand. Place a mound of blue cheese on each plate and sprinkle with chopped almonds. Drizzle the figs very lightly with the olive oil.

blinis with prawns & wasabi cream

SERVES 6

350 g/12 oz plain flour

125 g/4½ oz buckwheat flour

2 tsp easy-blend dried yeast

600 ml/1 pint milk, warmed

6 eggs, separated

3 tbsp unsalted butter, melted

5 tbsp soured cream

50 g/1¾ oz clarified butter

wasabi cream

200 ml/7 fl oz soured cream or crème fraîche

½ tsp wasabi paste, or to taste

salt

to serve

300 g/10½ oz cooked prawns, peeled and deveined

50 g/1¾ oz pickled ginger, thinly sliced

2 tbsp fresh coriander leaves

1 Sift the flours together into a large bowl and stir in the yeast. Make a hollow in the centre and add the milk, then gradually beat in the flour until you have a smooth batter. Cover and chill in the refrigerator overnight.

2 Two hours before you need the blinis, remove the bowl from the refrigerator and leave the batter for 1 hour 20 minutes to return to room temperature. Beat in the egg yolks, melted butter and soured cream. In a separate bowl, whisk the egg whites until stiff, then gradually fold into the batter. Cover and leave to rest for 30 minutes.

3 Meanwhile, make the wasabi cream. Mix the soured cream and wasabi paste together in a small bowl until completely combined. Taste and add a little more wasabi paste if you like it hotter. Season to taste with salt, cover and chill in the refrigerator.

4 To cook the blinis, heat a little of the clarified butter in a non-stick frying pan over a medium–high heat. When hot and sizzling, drop in 3–4 tablespoonfuls of the batter, spaced well apart, and cook until puffed up and tiny bubbles appear around the edges. Flip them over and cook for a few more minutes on the other side. Remove from the pan and keep warm while you cook the remaining batter.

5 To serve, spoon a little of the wasabi cream on to a blini, add 1 or 2 prawns and a little ginger, then scatter with a few coriander leaves.

piquant crab bites

MAKES 50

100 g/3½ oz fresh white breadcrumbs

2 large eggs, separated

200 ml/7 fl oz crème fraîche

1 tsp English mustard powder

500 g/1 lb 2 oz fresh white crabmeat

1 tbsp chopped fresh dill

groundnut oil, for frying

salt and pepper

2 limes, quartered, to serve

1 Tip the breadcrumbs into a large bowl. In a separate bowl, whisk the egg yolks with the crème fraîche and mustard powder and add to the breadcrumbs with the crabmeat and dill, season to taste with salt and pepper and mix together well. Cover and chill in the refrigerator for 15 minutes.

2 In a clean bowl, whisk the egg whites until stiff. Lightly fold a tablespoonful of the egg whites into the crab mixture, then fold in the remaining egg whites.

3 Heat 2 tablespoons of oil in a non-stick frying pan over a medium–high heat. Drop in as many teaspoonfuls of the crab mixture as will fit in the frying pan without overcrowding, flatten slightly and cook for 2 minutes, or until brown and crisp. Flip over and cook for a further 1–2 minutes until the undersides are browned. Remove and drain on kitchen paper. Keep warm while you cook the remaining crab mixture, adding more oil to the frying pan if necessary.

4 Serve the crab bites warm with the lime quarters for squeezing over.

VARIATION

Instead of crabmeat, use cooked flaked salmon. Omit the mustard powder and add a good pinch of cayenne pepper to the mix. Serve with lemon quarters instead of lime.

Main

Courses

roast turkey

SERVES 8

1 quantity Chestnut & Sausage Stuffing (see page 138)

1 turkey, weighing 5 kg/11 lb

40 g/1½ oz butter

bay and sage leaves, to garnish

to serve

Bread Sauce (see page 144)

Perfect Roast Potatoes (see page 110)

Spiced Winter Vegetables (see page 126)

1 Preheat the oven to 220°C/425°F/Gas Mark 7. Spoon one quantity of Chestnut & Sausage Stuffing into the neck cavity of the turkey and close the flap of skin with a skewer. Place the bird in a large roasting tin and rub it all over with the butter. Roast in the preheated oven for 1 hour, then lower the oven temperature to 180°C/350°F/Gas Mark 4 and roast for a further 2½ hours. You may need to pour off the fat from the roasting tin occasionally.

2 Check that the turkey is cooked by inserting a skewer or the point of a sharp knife into the thickest part of the thigh – if the juices run clear, it is ready. Transfer the bird to a carving board, cover loosely with foil and leave to rest.

3 Garnish the turkey with bay and sage leaves. Carve and serve with the warm bread sauce, roast potatoes and vegetables.

yuletide goose with honey & pears

SERVES 4–6

**1 goose, weighing
3.5–4.5 kg/7¾–10 lb**

1 tsp salt

4 pears

1 tbsp lemon juice

55 g/2 oz butter

2 tbsp honey

1 Preheat the oven to 220°C/425°F/Gas Mark 7. Use a fork to prick the skin of the goose all over, then rub with the salt. Place the bird upside down on a rack in a roasting tin. Roast in the preheated oven for 30 minutes. Drain off the fat. Turn the bird over and roast for 15 minutes. Drain off the fat.

2 Reduce the heat to 180°C/350°F/Gas Mark 4 and roast for 15 minutes per 450 g/1 lb. Cover with foil 15 minutes before the end of the cooking time. Check that the bird is cooked by inserting a knife between the legs and body. If the juices run clear, it is cooked. Remove from the oven. Transfer the goose to a warmed serving platter, cover loosely with foil and leave to rest.

3 Peel and halve the pears, then brush with the lemon juice. Melt the butter and honey in a saucepan over a low heat, then add the pears. Cook, stirring, for 5–10 minutes until tender. Remove from the heat, arrange the pears around the goose and pour the sweet juices over the bird, then serve.

roast duck with apple wedges

SERVES 4

4 duckling portions, about 350 g/12 oz each

4 tbsp dark soy sauce

2 tbsp light muscovado sugar

2 red-skinned apples

2 green-skinned apples

juice of 1 lemon

2 tbsp clear honey

a few bay leaves

salt and pepper

freshly cooked vegetables, to serve

apricot sauce

400 g/14 oz canned apricots in fruit juice

4 tbsp sweet sherry

1 Preheat the oven to 190°C/375°F/Gas Mark 5. Trim away any excess fat on the duck. Place on a wire rack over a roasting tin and prick all over with a fork or a clean, sharp needle.

2 Brush the duck with the soy sauce. Sprinkle over the sugar and season with pepper. Cook in the preheated oven, basting occasionally, for 50–60 minutes, or until the meat is cooked through and the juices run clear when a skewer is inserted into the thickest part of the meat.

3 Meanwhile, core the apples and cut each into 6 wedges, then place in a small bowl and mix with the lemon juice and honey. Transfer to a small roasting tin, add a few bay leaves and season to taste with salt and pepper. Cook alongside the duck, basting occasionally, for 20–25 minutes until tender. Discard the bay leaves.

4 To make the sauce, place the apricots in a blender or food processor with the can juices and the sherry. Process until smooth. Alternatively, mash the apricots with a fork until smooth and mix with the juice and sherry.

5 Just before serving, heat the apricot sauce in a small saucepan. Serve the duck with the apple wedges, apricot sauce and freshly cooked vegetables.

duck with madeira & blueberry sauce

SERVES 4

4 duck breasts (skin left on)

4 garlic cloves, chopped

grated rind and juice of 1 orange

1 tbsp chopped fresh parsley

salt and pepper

selection of green vegetables, to serve

madeira & blueberry sauce

150 g/5½ oz blueberries

250 ml/9 fl oz Madeira

1 tbsp redcurrant jelly

1 Use a sharp knife to make several shallow diagonal cuts in each duck breast. Put the duck in a glass bowl with the garlic, orange rind and juice, and the parsley. Season to taste with salt and pepper and stir well. Turn the duck in the mixture until thoroughly coated. Cover the bowl with clingfilm and leave in the refrigerator to marinate for at least 1 hour.

2 Heat a dry, non-stick frying pan over a medium heat. Add the duck breasts and cook for 4 minutes, then turn them over and cook for a further 4 minutes, or according to taste. Remove from the heat, cover the frying pan and leave to stand for 5 minutes.

3 To make the sauce, halfway through the cooking time, put the blueberries, Madeira and redcurrant jelly into a separate saucepan. Bring to the boil. Reduce the heat and simmer for 10 minutes, then remove from the heat.

4 Slice the duck breasts and transfer to warmed serving plates. Serve with the sauce poured over and accompanied by a selection of green vegetables.

roast pheasant with wine & herbs

SERVES 4

100 g/3½ oz butter, slightly softened

1 tbsp chopped fresh thyme

1 tbsp chopped fresh parsley

2 oven-ready young pheasants

4 tbsp vegetable oil

125 ml/4 fl oz red wine

salt and pepper

game chips, to serve

1 Preheat the oven to 190°C/375°F/Gas Mark 5. Put the butter in a small bowl and mix in the chopped herbs. Lift the skin away from the breasts of the pheasants, taking care not to tear it, and push the herb butter under the skins. Season to taste with salt and pepper. Pour the oil into a roasting tin, add the pheasants and roast in the preheated oven for 45 minutes, basting occasionally.

2 Remove from the oven, pour over the wine, then return to the oven and cook for a further 15 minutes, or until cooked through. Check that each bird is cooked by inserting a knife between the legs and body. If the juices run clear, they are cooked.

3 Remove the pheasants from the oven, cover loosely with foil and leave to rest for 15 minutes. Serve on a warmed serving platter surrounded by game chips.

quail with grapes

SERVES 4

4 tbsp olive oil

8 quail, gutted

280 g/10 oz green seedless grapes

225 ml/8 fl oz grape juice

2 cloves

about 150 ml/5 fl oz water

2 tbsp brandy

salt and pepper

potato pancake

600 g/1 lb 5 oz unpeeled potatoes

35 g/1¼ oz unsalted butter or pork fat

1½ tbsp olive oil

salt and pepper

1 Preheat the oven to 230°C/450°F/Gas Mark 8. For the pancake, parboil the potatoes for 10 minutes. Drain and leave to cool completely, then peel, coarsely grate and season with salt and pepper to taste. Reserve until required.

2 Take a heavy-based frying pan or flameproof casserole large enough to hold the quail in a single layer and heat the oil over a medium heat. Add the quail and fry on all sides until they are golden brown.

3 Add the grapes, grape juice, cloves, enough water to come halfway up the side of the quail, and salt and pepper to taste. Cover and simmer for 20 minutes. Transfer the quail and all the juices to a roasting tin or casserole, and sprinkle with brandy. Roast, uncovered, in the preheated oven for 10 minutes.

4 Meanwhile, to make the potato pancake, melt the butter with the oil in a 30-cm/12-inch non-stick frying pan over a high heat. When the fat is hot, add the grated potato and spread into an even layer. Reduce the heat and fry for 10 minutes. Turn the pancake over and continue cooking on the other side until cooked through and crisp. Slide out of the frying pan and cut into 4 wedges. Keep the pancake warm until the quail are ready.

5 Place a pancake wedge and 2 quail on each individual serving plate. Taste the grape sauce and adjust the seasoning, adding salt and pepper if necessary. Spoon the sauce over the quail and serve immediately.

traditional roast chicken

SERVES 6

1 chicken, weighing 2.25 kg/5 lb

55 g/2 oz butter

2 tbsp chopped fresh lemon thyme

2 lemons, halved

125 ml/4 fl oz white wine

salt and pepper

fresh thyme sprigs, to garnish

1 Preheat the oven to 220°C/425°F/Gas Mark 7. Make sure the chicken is clean, wiping it inside and out with kitchen paper, and place in a roasting tin. In a bowl, soften the butter with a fork, mix in the thyme and season well with salt and pepper. Butter the chicken all over with the herb butter, inside and out, and place the lemon pieces inside the body cavity. Pour the wine over the chicken.

2 Roast in the centre of the preheated oven for 20 minutes. Reduce the temperature to 190°C/375°F/Gas Mark 5 and roast for a further 1¼ hours, basting frequently. Cover with foil if the skin begins to brown too much. If the tin dries out, add a little more wine or water.

3 Test that the chicken is cooked by piercing the thickest part of the leg with a sharp knife or skewer and making sure the juices run clear. Remove from the oven. Transfer the chicken to a warmed serving dish, cover loosely with foil and leave to rest for 10 minutes before carving. Remove the lemon halves and place around the sides of the dish. Place the roasting tin on the top of the stove and bubble the pan juices gently over a low heat until they have reduced and are thick and glossy. Season to taste with salt and pepper. Serve the chicken with the pan juices and scatter with the thyme sprigs.

chicken roulades

SERVES 6

6 skinless, boneless chicken breasts, about 175 g/6 oz each

200 g/7 oz fresh chicken mince

1 tbsp olive oil

2 shallots, roughly chopped

1 garlic clove, crushed

150 ml/5 fl oz double cream

3 fresh sage leaves, chopped

1 tbsp chopped fresh parsley

1 tbsp brandy or sherry

1 tbsp vegetable oil

18 pancetta rashers

1 dessertspoon plain flour

200 ml/7 fl oz white wine

200 ml/7 fl oz chicken stock

salt and pepper

freshly cooked vegetables, to serve

1 Place each chicken breast between clingfilm and flatten with a rolling pin as evenly as possible. Trim neatly and chill. Chop the chicken trimmings and mix with the mince in a bowl. Heat the olive oil in a frying pan over a medium heat, add the shallots and garlic and cook for 5 minutes. Add to the mince with the cream, herbs and brandy and mix together well. Season to taste with salt and pepper, cover and chill for 15 minutes.

2 Divide the mince mixture between the breasts, spread to within 1 cm/½ inch of the edge, and then roll each breast up. Wrap each roll securely in kitchen foil. Poach in a large pan of simmering water for 20 minutes, remove with a slotted spoon and cool completely.

3 Preheat the oven to 190°C/375°F/Gas Mark 5. Heat the vegetable oil in a roasting tin in the oven. Remove the foil and wrap each roulade tightly in 3 pancetta rashers. Roll them in the hot oil, then roast in the oven for 25–30 minutes, turning twice, until they are browned and crisp.

4 Remove the roulades and keep warm. Place the tin on the hob, add the flour and stir well to form a smooth paste. Gradually whisk in the wine and stock. Simmer for 4–5 minutes, then season to taste. Serve the roulades sliced with the gravy and vegetables.

prime rib of beef au jus

SERVES 8

2.7 kg/6 lb rib of beef
55 g/2 oz butter, softened
1½ tsp sea salt flakes
1 tbsp ground black pepper
2 tbsp flour
1 litre/1¾ pints beef stock
thyme sprigs, to garnish
roast potatoes and
vegetables, to serve

1 Place the beef bone-side down in a deep-sided roasting tin. Rub the entire surface of the meat with butter, and coat evenly with the salt and black pepper.

2 Leave the beef to reach room temperature for 1 hour. Preheat the oven to 230°C/450°F/Gas Mark 8. Place the meat in the preheated oven and allow to roast uncovered for 20 minutes to sear the outside of the roast.

3 Reduce the heat to 160°C/325°F/Gas Mark 3 and roast for 15 minutes per pound of meat for medium-rare (plus or minus 15 minutes for well done and rare respectively). Transfer the meat to a large platter and cover with foil. Allow to rest for 30 minutes before serving.

4 Pour off all but 2 tablespoons of the fat from the pan and place the roasting tin over a medium heat. Add the flour to the roasting pan and simmer, stirring with a wooden spoon for 1 minute to form a thick paste. Pour in a ladleful of beef stock, bring to the boil, stirring and scraping all the caramelized beef drippings from the bottom of the pan. Repeat with the remaining stock, a ladleful at a time. Simmer for 10 minutes.

5 Serve the beef with the 'jus' accompanied by roast potatoes and vegetables and garnished with thyme sprigs.

festive beef wellington

SERVES 4

750 g/1 lb 10 oz thick beef fillet

2 tbsp butter

2 tbsp vegetable oil

1 garlic clove, chopped

1 onion, chopped

175 g/6 oz chestnut mushrooms, thinly sliced

1 tbsp chopped fresh sage

350 g/12 oz puff pastry, thawed if frozen

1 egg, beaten

salt and pepper

1 Preheat the oven to 220°C/425°F/Gas Mark 7. Put the beef in a roasting tin, spread with the butter and season to taste with salt and pepper. Roast in the preheated oven for 30 minutes, then remove from the oven.

2 Meanwhile, heat the oil in a saucepan over a medium heat. Add the garlic and onion and cook, stirring, for 3 minutes. Stir in salt and pepper to taste, the mushrooms and the sage and cook, stirring frequently, for 5 minutes. Remove from the heat.

3 Roll out the pastry into a rectangle large enough to enclose the beef, then place the beef in the centre and spread the mushroom mixture over it. Bring the long sides of the pastry together over the beef and seal with beaten egg. Tuck the short ends over (trim away excess pastry) and seal. Place on a baking sheet, seam-side down. Make 2 slits in the top. Decorate with pastry shapes and brush with egg. Bake for 40 minutes. Remove from the oven, cut into thick slices and serve.

steak with pancakes & mustard sauce

SERVES 6

6 fillet steaks, about 150 g/5½ oz each

1 tbsp olive oil

1 tsp unsalted butter

200 ml/7 fl oz crème fraîche

2 tsp wholegrain mustard

salt and pepper

2 tbsp snipped fresh chives, to garnish

pancakes

400 g/14 oz potatoes

55 g/2 oz self-raising flour

½ tsp baking powder

200 ml/7 fl oz milk

2 eggs, beaten

vegetable oil, for frying

1 To make the pancakes, cook the potatoes in their skins in a large saucepan of boiling water until tender. Drain and leave until cool enough to handle. Peel, then pass through a potato ricer, or mash and press through a sieve, into a bowl.

2 Sift the flour and baking powder over the potatoes, then add a little of the milk and mix well. Add the remaining milk and the eggs and beat well to make a smooth batter.

3 Heat a little vegetable oil in a 20-cm/8-inch non-stick frying pan over a medium heat. Add a ladleful of the batter to cover the base of the pan and cook until little bubbles appear on the surface. Turn over and cook for a further minute, or until nicely browned, then turn out and keep warm. Repeat until you have cooked 6 pancakes.

4 Season the steaks to taste with salt and pepper. Heat the olive oil and butter in a non-stick frying pan over a high heat until sizzling. Add the fillet steaks and cook to your liking, then remove from the pan and keep warm. Add the crème fraîche and mustard to the pan, stir and heat through. Season well with salt and pepper. Serve each steak with a folded pancake and some sauce, scattered with a few snipped chives.

roast venison with brandy sauce

SERVES 6

6 tbsp vegetable oil

1.7 kg/3 lb 12 oz saddle of fresh venison, trimmed

salt and pepper

freshly cooked vegetables, to serve

brandy sauce

1 tbsp plain flour

4 tbsp vegetable stock

175 ml/6 fl oz brandy

100 ml/3½ fl oz double cream

1 Preheat the oven to 180°C/350°F/Gas Mark 4. Heat half the oil in a frying pan over a high heat.

2 Season the venison to taste with salt and pepper, add to the pan and cook until lightly browned all over. Pour the remaining oil into a roasting pan. Add the venison, cover with foil and roast in the preheated oven, basting occasionally, for 1½ hours, or until cooked through. Remove from the oven and transfer to a warmed serving platter. Cover with foil and set aside.

3 To make the sauce, stir the flour into the roasting pan over the hob and cook for 1 minute. Pour in the stock and heat it, stirring to loosen the sediment from the base. Gradually stir in the brandy and bring to the boil, then reduce the heat and simmer, stirring, for 10–15 minutes until the sauce has thickened a little. Remove from the heat and stir in the cream.

4 Serve the venison with the brandy sauce and a selection of freshly cooked vegetables.

glazed gammon

SERVES 8

**1 gammon joint,
weighing 4 kg/8¾ lb**

1 apple, cored and chopped

1 onion, chopped

300 ml/10 fl oz dry cider

6 black peppercorns

1 bouquet garni

1 bay leaf

about 50 cloves

4 tbsp demerara sugar

1 Put the gammon in a large saucepan and add enough cold water to cover. Bring to the boil and skim off the foam that rises to the surface. Reduce the heat and simmer for 30 minutes. Drain the gammon and return to the saucepan. Add the apple, onion, cider, peppercorns, bouquet garni, bay leaf and a few of the cloves. Pour in enough fresh water to cover and return to the boil. Reduce the heat, cover and simmer for 3 hours 20 minutes.

2 Preheat the oven to 200°C/400°F/Gas Mark 6. Take the saucepan off the heat and set aside to cool slightly. Remove the gammon from the cooking liquid and, while it is still warm, loosen the rind with a sharp knife, then peel it off and discard. Score the fat into diamond shapes and stud with the remaining cloves. Place the gammon on a rack in a roasting tin and sprinkle with the sugar. Roast in the oven for 20 minutes, basting occasionally with the cooking liquid. Serve hot, or cold later.

roast pork loin

SERVES 6

1.8 kg/4 lb flat piece pork loin, chined (backbone removed) and rind scored

3 garlic cloves, crushed

2 tbsp chopped fresh rosemary

4 sprigs fresh rosemary, plus extra to garnish

225 ml/8 fl oz dry white wine

salt and pepper

cooked seasonal vegetables, to serve (optional)

1 Preheat the oven to 230°C/450°F/Gas Mark 8. Put the pork loin on a work surface, skin-side down. Make small slits in the meat all over the surface. Season very well with salt and pepper. Rub the garlic all over the meat surface and sprinkle with the chopped rosemary.

2 Roll up the loin and secure 4 rosemary sprigs on the outside with fine string. Make sure that the joint is securely tied. Season the rind with plenty of salt to give a good crackling.

3 Transfer the meat to a roasting tin and roast in the preheated oven for 20 minutes, or until the fat has started to run. Reduce the oven temperature to 190°C/375°F/Gas Mark 5 and pour half the wine over the meat. Roast for a further 1 hour 40 minutes, basting occasionally with the pan juices.

4 Remove the meat from the oven and leave to rest in a warm place for 15 minutes before carving. Remove the string and rosemary before cutting into thick slices.

5 Pour off all but 1 tablespoon of the fat from the roasting tin. Add the remaining wine to the juices in the tin and bring to the boil, scraping up and stirring in any residue from the base of the tin. Spoon over the meat and serve immediately with fresh vegetables, if using, and garnished with extra sprigs of rosemary.

lamb with roquefort & walnut butter

SERVES 4

55 g/2 oz butter

140 g/5 oz Roquefort cheese, crumbled

2 tbsp finely chopped walnuts

8 lamb noisettes

salt and pepper

snipped chives, to garnish (optional)

freshly cooked vegetables, to serve

1 Cream half the butter in a bowl with a wooden spoon. Beat in the cheese and walnuts until thoroughly combined and season to taste with salt and pepper. Turn out the flavoured butter onto a sheet of greaseproof paper and shape into a cylinder. Wrap and leave to chill in the refrigerator until firm.

2 Heat a ridged griddle pan, add the remaining butter and as soon as it has melted, add the lamb noisettes. Then cook for 4–5 minutes on each side.

3 Transfer the lamb to warmed serving plates and top each noisette with a slice of Roquefort and walnut butter. Serve immediately with snipped chives, to garnish, if using, and freshly cooked vegetables.

roast monkfish with boulangère potatoes

SERVES 4

40 g/1½ oz butter, melted

700 g/1 lb 9 oz floury potatoes peeled and, very thinly sliced

1 onion, very thinly sliced

1 tbsp roughly chopped fresh thyme

about 200 ml/7 fl oz vegetable stock

4 skinless monkfish fillets, about 200 g/7 oz each

4 tbsp olive oil

finely pared rind of 1 lemon

8 tbsp chopped fresh flat-leaf parsley

1 garlic clove, crushed

salt and pepper

mixed rocket, watercress and baby spinach leaves, to serve

1 Preheat the oven to 200°C/400°F/Gas Mark 6. Brush a shallow ovenproof dish with a little of the melted butter. Layer the potatoes, onion and thyme in the dish, seasoning well with salt and pepper between the layers and finishing with a layer of potatoes.

2 Pour in enough of the stock to come halfway up the potatoes and drizzle the remaining melted butter over the top. Bake in the centre of the preheated oven for 40–50 minutes, pressing the potatoes into the stock once or twice with the back of a spatula until tender and browned on top.

3 Season the monkfish well with salt and pepper. Mix together the oil, lemon rind, parsley and garlic and rub all over the monkfish. Sear the monkfish in a smoking hot frying pan or on a griddle pan for 1 minute on each side, or until browned. Transfer the monkfish to a roasting tin, spaced well apart, and roast on the top shelf of the oven for the final 12–15 minutes of the cooking time, until just cooked through. Serve immediately with the potatoes and mixed salad leaves.

herbed salmon with hollandaise sauce

SERVES 4

4 salmon fillets, about 175 g/6 oz each, skin removed

2 tbsp olive oil

1 tbsp chopped fresh dill

1 tbsp snipped fresh chives, plus extra to garnish

salt and pepper

freshly cooked sprouting broccoli and sesame seeds, to serve

hollandaise sauce

3 egg yolks

1 tbsp water

225 g/8 oz butter, cut into small cubes

juice of 1 lemon

salt and pepper

1 Preheat the grill to medium. Rinse the fish fillets under cold running water and pat dry with kitchen paper. Season to taste with salt and pepper. Combine the oil with the dill and chives in a bowl, then brush the mixture over the fish. Transfer to the grill and cook for 6–8 minutes, turning once and brushing with more oil and herb mixture, until cooked to your taste.

2 Meanwhile, make the sauce. Put the egg yolks in a heatproof bowl over a saucepan of gently simmering water (or use a double boiler). Add the water and season to taste with salt and pepper. Reduce the heat until the water in the saucepan is barely simmering and whisk constantly until the mixture begins to thicken. Whisk in the butter, one piece at a time, until the mixture is thick and shiny. Whisk in the lemon juice, then remove from the heat.

3 Remove the salmon from the grill and transfer to warmed individual serving plates. Pour the sauce over the fish and garnish with snipped fresh chives. Serve immediately on a bed of sprouting broccoli, garnished with sesame seeds.

poached salmon

SERVES 8–12

4 litres/7 pints water

6 tbsp white wine vinegar

1 large onion, sliced

2 carrots, sliced

1½ tbsp salt

1 tsp black peppercorns

1 whole salmon, weighing 2.7kg/6 lb, cleaned with gills and eyes removed

fresh dill, to garnish

salad, to serve

1 To make a court-bouillon (stock) in which to poach the fish, put the water, vinegar, onion, carrots, salt and peppercorns in a large fish kettle or covered roasting tin and bring to the boil. Reduce the heat and simmer for 20 minutes. Remove the trivet (if using a fish kettle) and lay the salmon on it. Lower it into the court-bouillon, cover, return to simmering point and cook for 5 minutes. Turn off the heat and leave the fish, covered, to cool in the liquid.

2 When the fish is cold, lift it out of the kettle on the trivet and drain well. Using two fish slices, carefully transfer to a board. Using a sharp knife, remove the head, then slit the skin along the backbone and peel off. Carefully turn the fish over and peel off the skin on the other side. Garnish with dill and serve with salad.

smoked salmon risotto

SERVES 4

50 g/1¾ oz unsalted butter

1 onion, finely chopped

½ small fennel bulb, very finely chopped

500 g/1 lb 2 oz arborio or carnaroli rice

300 ml/10 fl oz white wine or vermouth

1.2 litres/2 pints hot fish stock

150 g/5½ oz hot-smoked salmon flakes

150 g/5½ oz smoked salmon slices

salt and pepper

2 tbsp fresh chervil leaves or chopped flat-leaf parsley, to garnish

1 Melt half the butter in a large saucepan over a medium heat, add the onion and fennel and cook, stirring frequently, for 5–8 minutes until transparent and soft. Add the rice and stir well to coat the grains in the butter. Cook, stirring, for 3 minutes, then add the wine, stir and leave to simmer until most of the liquid has been absorbed.

2 With the stock simmering in a separate saucepan, add 1 ladleful to the rice and stir well. Cook, stirring constantly, until nearly all the liquid has been absorbed before adding another ladleful of stock. Continue to add the remaining stock in the same way until the rice is cooked al dente and most or all of the stock has been added.

3 Remove from the heat and stir in the hot-smoked salmon and the remaining butter, season to taste with salt and pepper. Serve with the smoked salmon on top and garnished with the chervil.

seafood pie with stilton

SERVES 6

300 ml/10 fl oz vegetable stock

100 ml/3½ fl oz dry vermouth

3 tbsp cornflour, blended with 3 tbsp cold water

30 g/1 oz butter, cut into small pieces

6 tbsp crème fraîche

375 g/13 oz skinless cod fillet, cut into chunks

375 g/13 oz skinless salmon fillet, cut into chunks

225 g/8 oz raw king prawns, peeled, deveined

175 g/6 oz fine asparagus spears, tough ends snapped off, cut into 2.5-cm/1-inch pieces

115 g/4 oz Stilton cheese, crumbled

4 tbsp snipped fresh chives

500 g/1 lb 2oz ready-made puff pastry

plain flour, for dusting

pepper

1 Pour the stock and vermouth into a saucepan and bring to the boil. Whisk in the cornflour paste and simmer for 1 minute to make a thick sauce. Remove from heat and stir in the butter and crème fraîche, then cover the surface with baking paper. Leave to cool.

2 Preheat the oven to 220°C/425°F/Gas Mark 7. Stir the fish, prawns, asparagus, Stilton and chives into the sauce. Season to taste with pepper, then spoon into a 1.4-litre/2½-pint pie dish.

3 Roll out the pastry on a lightly floured surface to a thickness of about 3 mm/⅛ inch. Cut a long 2-cm/¾-inch strip and press around the rim of the pie dish, fixing it in place with a little water. Use the remaining pastry to cover the pie, cutting the trimmings into shapes to decorate and fixing into place with a little water. Make a small hole in the centre to allow steam to escape.

4 Bake in the preheated oven for 20 minutes, until the pastry is well risen and golden brown, then reduce the temperate to 180°C/350°F/Gas Mark 4 and bake for a further 35 minutes. Serve immediately.

mixed nut roast

SERVES 4

25 g/1 oz butter, plus extra for greasing

2 garlic cloves, chopped

1 large onion, chopped

50 g/1¾ oz pine kernels, toasted

75 g/2¾ oz hazelnuts, toasted

50 g/1¾ oz walnuts, ground

50 g/1¾ oz cashew nuts, ground

100 g/3½ oz fresh wholemeal breadcrumbs

1 egg, lightly beaten

2 tbsp chopped fresh thyme

250 ml/9 fl oz vegetable stock

salt and pepper

fresh thyme sprigs, to garnish

cranberry sauce, to serve

1 Preheat the oven to 180°C/350°F/Gas Mark 4. Grease a loaf tin with butter and line it with greaseproof paper. Melt the remaining butter in a saucepan over a medium heat. Add the garlic and onion and cook, stirring, for 5 minutes, until softened. Remove from the heat. Grind the pine kernels and hazelnuts. Stir all the nuts into the saucepan, add the breadcrumbs, egg, thyme and stock and season to taste with salt and pepper.

2 Spoon the mixture into the loaf tin and level the surface. Cook in the preheated oven for 30 minutes, or until cooked through and golden. The loaf is cooked when a skewer inserted into the centre comes out clean.

3 Remove the nut roast from the oven and turn out onto a warmed serving dish. Garnish with thyme sprigs and serve with cranberry sauce.

roast squash with cranberries

SERVES 4

4 acorn or 2 small butternut squash

100 g/3½ oz basmati rice

50 g/1¾ oz wild rice

25 g/1 oz butter, plus extra for dotting

1 tbsp olive oil, plus extra for oiling

1 red onion, thinly sliced

2 garlic cloves, crushed

100 g/3½ oz dried cranberries

50 g/1¾ oz pine kernels, toasted

2 tbsp finely chopped fresh parsley

pinch of freshly grated nutmeg

70 g/2½ oz fresh white or wholemeal breadcrumbs

25 g/1 oz finely grated Parmesan cheese

salt and pepper

1 If using acorn squash, cut through the centre and trim the stalk and root so that the squash will stand upright securely, then scoop out and discard the seeds. If using butternut squash, cut lengthways in half and scoop out and discard the seeds. Place the prepared squash on an oiled baking sheet.

2 Cook the two types of rice separately according to the packet instructions and drain well.

3 Meanwhile, preheat the oven to 190°C/375°F/Gas Mark 5. Melt the butter with the oil in a frying pan over a medium heat, add the onion and garlic and cook, stirring frequently, for 8 minutes, or until transparent and soft.

4 Tip all the cooked rice and the cooked onion and garlic into a bowl. Add the cranberries, pine kernels and parsley, grate in a little nutmeg and season to taste with salt and pepper. Mix together well.

5 Carefully divide the stuffing mixture between the squash, then top with the breadcrumbs and Parmesan cheese and dot with butter. Bake in the preheated oven for 50 minutes, then serve hot.

wild mushroom filo parcels

SERVES 6

30 g/1 oz dried porcini mushrooms

70 g/2½ oz butter

1 shallot, finely chopped

1 garlic clove, crushed

100 g/3½ oz chestnut mushrooms, sliced

100 g/3½ oz white cap mushrooms, sliced

200 g/7 oz wild mushrooms, roughly chopped

150 g/5½ oz basmati rice, cooked and cooled

2 tbsp dry sherry

1 tbsp soy sauce or mushroom sauce

1 tbsp chopped fresh flat-leaf parsley

18 sheets filo pastry, thawed if frozen

vegetable oil, for oiling

salt and pepper

sauce

350 ml/12 fl oz crème fraîche

50 ml/2 fl oz Madeira

salt and pepper

1 Just cover the dried mushrooms with boiling water and soak for 20 minutes. Drain and reserve the liquid.

2 Melt half the butter in a large frying pan over a low heat, add the shallot and garlic and cook, stirring, for 5–8 minutes until the shallot is transparent and soft. Add the fresh mushrooms and cook, stirring, for 2–3 minutes. Roughly chop the drained mushrooms and add to the frying pan with the rice, sherry, soy sauce and parsley. Season well with salt and pepper, mix together and simmer until most of the liquid has evaporated.

3 Preheat the oven to 200°C/400°F/Gas Mark 6. Melt the remaining butter in a small saucepan. Lay one sheet of filo pastry on a work surface and brush with melted butter. Put another sheet on top and brush with butter, then top with a third sheet. Spoon some of the mushroom mixture into the centre, then fold in the edges to form a parcel. Secure the edges with a little butter. Repeat to make 6 parcels. Place the parcels on a lightly oiled baking sheet and brush with the remaining melted butter. Bake in the preheated oven for 25–30 minutes until golden.

4 To make the sauce, heat the reserved soaking liquid in a saucepan, add the crème fraîche and Madeira and stir over a low heat until heated through. Season to taste with salt and pepper and serve with the parcels.

cheese & vegetable tart

SERVES 6

350 g/12 oz ready-made shortcrust pastry, thawed if frozen

plain flour, for dusting

280 g/10 oz mixed frozen vegetables

150 ml/5 fl oz double cream

115 g/4 oz Cheddar cheese, grated

salt and pepper

1 Thinly roll out the dough on a lightly floured work surface and use to line a 23-cm/9-inch quiche tin. Prick the base and chill in the refrigerator for 30 minutes. Preheat the oven to 200°C/400°F/Gas Mark 6.

2 Line the pastry case with foil and half-fill with baking beans. Place the tin on a baking sheet and bake for 15–20 minutes, or until just firm. Remove the beans and foil, return the pastry case to the oven and bake for a further 5–7 minutes until golden. Remove the pastry case from the oven and leave to cool in the tin.

3 Meanwhile, cook the frozen vegetables in a saucepan of salted boiling water. Drain and leave to cool.

4 When ready to cook, preheat the oven again to 200°C/400°F/Gas Mark 6. Mix the cooked vegetables and cream together and season with salt and pepper. Spoon the mixture evenly into the pastry case and sprinkle with the cheese. Bake for 15 minutes, or until the cheese has melted and is turning golden. Serve hot or cold.

VARIATION

Crumble 100 g/3½ oz soft goat's cheese on top of the vegetable and cream mixture. Then, instead of the Cheddar, top with 2 teaspoons of grated Parmesan mixed with 1 teaspoon of toasted breadcrumbs.

Side Dishes

perfect roast potatoes

SERVES 8

70 g/2½ oz goose or duck fat or 5 tbsp olive oil

1 kg/2 lb 4 oz even-sized potatoes, peeled

coarse sea salt

8 fresh rosemary sprigs, to garnish

1 Preheat the oven to 230°C/450°F/Gas Mark 8. Put the fat in a large roasting tin, sprinkle generously with sea salt and place in the oven.

2 Meanwhile, cook the potatoes in a large saucepan of boiling water for 8–10 minutes until parboiled. Drain well and, if the potatoes are large, cut them in half. Return the potatoes to the empty saucepan and shake vigorously to roughen their outsides.

3 Arrange the potatoes in a single layer in the hot fat and roast for 45 minutes. If they look as if they are beginning to char around the edges, reduce the oven temperature to 200°C/400°F/Gas Mark 6. Turn the potatoes over and roast for a further 30 minutes until crisp. Serve garnished with rosemary sprigs.

potatoes dauphinois

SERVES 4

1 tbsp butter

675 g/1 lb 8 oz waxy potatoes, peeled and sliced

2 garlic cloves, crushed

1 red onion, sliced

85 g/3 oz Gruyère cheese, grated

300 ml/10 fl oz double cream

salt and pepper

1 Preheat the oven to 180°C/350°F/Gas Mark 4. Lightly grease a 1-litre/1¾-pint shallow ovenproof dish with the butter.

2 Arrange a single layer of potato slices evenly in the base of the prepared dish.

3 Top the potato slices with half the garlic, half the sliced red onion and one third of the grated Gruyère cheese. Season to taste with a little salt and some pepper.

4 Repeat the layers in exactly the same order, finishing with a layer of potatoes topped with grated cheese.

5 Pour the cream over the top of the potatoes and cook in the preheated oven for 1½ hours, or until the potatoes are cooked through and the top is browned and crispy. Serve at once, straight from the dish.

garlic mash

SERVES 4

900 g/2 lb floury potatoes, peeled and cut into chunks

8 garlic cloves, crushed

150 ml/5 fl oz milk

85 g/3 oz butter

pinch of freshly grated nutmeg

salt and pepper

1 Place the potatoes in a large saucepan with enough water to cover and a pinch of salt. Bring to the boil and cook for 10 minutes. Add the garlic and cook for a further 10–15 minutes, or until the potatoes are tender.

2 Drain the potatoes and garlic, reserving 3 tablespoons of the cooking liquid. Return the reserved cooking liquid to the saucepan, then add the milk and bring to simmering point. Add the butter, return the potatoes and garlic to the saucepan and turn off the heat. Mash thoroughly with a potato masher.

3 Season the potato mixture to taste with nutmeg, salt and pepper and beat thoroughly with a wooden spoon until light and fluffy. Serve immediately.

two-potato purée

SERVES 6

2 large orange sweet potatoes

½ tsp vegetable oil

4 potatoes, peeled

25 g/1 oz butter

125 ml/4 fl oz double cream

pinch of freshly grated nutmeg

salt and pepper

1 Preheat the oven to 190°C/375°F/Gas Mark 5. Rub the sweet potatoes with the oil, then bake in the preheated oven for 20–25 minutes until tender.

2 Meanwhile, cook the potatoes in a large saucepan of boiling water until tender. Drain well and put in a colander. Cover with a clean tea towel to absorb the steam. Mash the potatoes or pass through a potato ricer.

3 Scoop out the flesh from the sweet potatoes and mix well with the potato in a warmed bowl. Discard the sweet potato skins. Melt the butter with the cream in a small saucepan, then pour half over the potato mixture and beat well with a wooden spoon. Add the remaining cream mixture a little at a time until you achieve the consistency you like. Season to taste with salt and pepper, and add a pinch of nutmeg. Beat again, then serve.

buttered brussels sprouts with chestnuts

SERVES 4

350 g/12 oz Brussels sprouts

3 tbsp butter

100 g/3½ oz canned whole chestnuts, drained

pinch of grated nutmeg

salt and pepper

50 g/1¾ oz flaked almonds, to garnish

1 Bring a large saucepan of salted water to the boil. Add the Brussels sprouts and cook for 5 minutes. Drain thoroughly.

2 Melt the butter in a large saucepan over a medium heat. Add the Brussels sprouts and cook, stirring, for 3 minutes, then add the chestnuts and nutmeg. Season to taste with salt and pepper and stir well. Cook for a further 2 minutes, stirring, then remove from the heat. Transfer to a warmed serving dish, scatter over the almonds and serve.

sugar–glazed parsnips

SERVES 8
24 small parsnips
about 1 tsp salt
115 g/4 oz butter
115 g/4 oz soft brown sugar

1 Place the parsnips in a saucepan, add just enough water to cover, then add the salt. Bring to the boil, reduce the heat, cover and simmer for 20–25 minutes, until tender. Drain well.

2 Melt the butter in a heavy frying pan or wok. Add the parsnips and toss well. Sprinkle with the sugar, then cook, stirring frequently to prevent the sugar from sticking to the pan or burning. Cook the parsnips for 10–15 minutes, until golden and glazed. Transfer to a warm serving dish and serve immediately.

honey-glazed red cabbage with sultanas

SERVES 4

2 tbsp butter

1 garlic clove, chopped

650 g/1 lb 7 oz red cabbage, shredded

150 g/5½ oz sultanas

1 tbsp clear honey

100 ml/3½ fl oz red wine

100 ml/3½ fl oz water

1 Melt the butter in a large saucepan over a medium heat. Add the garlic and cook, stirring, for 1 minute, until slightly softened.

2 Add the cabbage and sultanas, then stir in the honey. Cook for 1 minute more. Pour in the wine and water and bring to the boil. Reduce the heat, cover and simmer gently, stirring occasionally, for 45 minutes, or until the cabbage is cooked. Serve hot.

cauliflower cheese

SERVES 4

1 cauliflower, cut into florets (675 g/1 lb 8 oz prepared weight)

40 g/1½ oz butter

40 g/1½ oz plain flour

450 ml/16 fl oz milk

115 g/4 oz Cheddar cheese, finely grated

pinch of freshly grated nutmeg

1 tbsp grated Parmesan cheese

salt and pepper

1 Cook the cauliflower in a saucepan of lightly salted boiling water for 4–5 minutes. It should still be firm. Drain, place in a preheated 1.4-litre/2½-pint gratin dish and keep warm.

2 Melt the butter in the rinsed-out saucepan over a medium heat and stir in the flour. Cook for 1 minute, stirring continuously. Remove from the heat and stir in the milk gradually until you have a smooth consistency.

3 Return to a medium heat and continue to stir while the sauce comes to the boil and thickens. Reduce the heat and simmer gently, stirring constantly, for about 3 minutes until the sauce is creamy and smooth.

4 Remove from the heat and stir in the Cheddar cheese and a good pinch of the grated nutmeg. Season to taste with salt and pepper.

5 Preheat the grill to high. Pour the sauce over the cauliflower, top with the Parmesan cheese and place under a hot grill to brown. Serve immediately.

spiced winter vegetables

SERVES 4

4 parsnips, scrubbed and trimmed but left unpeeled

4 carrots, scrubbed and trimmed but left unpeeled

2 onions, quartered

1 red onion, quartered

3 leeks, trimmed and cut into 6-cm/2½-inch slices

6 garlic cloves, left unpeeled and whole

6 tbsp extra virgin olive oil

½ tsp mild chilli powder

pinch of paprika

salt and pepper

1 Preheat the oven to 220°C/425°F/Gas Mark 7. Bring a large saucepan of water to the boil.

2 Cut the parsnips and carrots into wedges of similar size. Add them to the saucepan and cook for 5 minutes. Drain thoroughly and place in an ovenproof dish with the onions, leeks and garlic. Pour over the oil, sprinkle in the spices and salt and pepper to taste, then mix until all the vegetables are well coated.

3 Roast in the preheated oven for at least 1 hour. Turn the vegetables from time to time until they are tender and starting to colour. Remove from the oven, transfer to a warmed serving dish and serve immediately.

roasted onions

SERVES 4

8 large onions

3 tbsp olive oil

55 g/2 oz butter

2 tsp chopped fresh thyme

**200 g/7 oz Cheddar cheese
or Lancashire cheese,
grated**

salt and pepper

1 Preheat the oven to 180°C/350°F/Gas Mark 4. Cut a cross down through the top of the onions towards the root, without cutting all the way through. Place the onions in a roasting tin and drizzle over the olive oil.

2 Press a little of the butter into the open crosses, sprinkle with the thyme and season with salt and pepper. Cover with foil and roast in the preheated oven for 40–45 minutes.

3 Remove from the oven, take off the foil and baste the onions with the pan juices. Return to the oven and cook for a further 15 minutes, uncovered, to allow the onions to brown.

4 Take the onions out of the oven and scatter the grated cheese over them. Return them to the oven for a few minutes so that the cheese starts to melt. Serve immediately.

garlic mushrooms with white wine & chestnuts

SERVES 4

55 g/2 oz butter

4 garlic cloves, chopped

200 g/7 oz button mushrooms, sliced

200 g/7 oz chestnut mushrooms, sliced

4 tbsp dry white wine

100 ml/3½ fl oz double cream

300 g/10½ oz canned whole chestnuts, drained

100 g/3½ oz chanterelle mushrooms, sliced

salt and pepper

chopped fresh parsley, to garnish

1 Melt the butter in a large saucepan over a medium heat. Add the garlic and cook, stirring, for 3 minutes, until softened. Add the button and chestnut mushrooms and cook for 3 minutes.

2 Stir in the wine and cream and season to taste with salt and pepper. Cook for 2 minutes, stirring, then add the chestnuts and the chanterelle mushrooms. Cook for a further 2 minutes, stirring, then remove from the heat and transfer to a warmed serving dish. Garnish with chopped fresh parsley and serve.

bacon-wrapped sausages

SERVES 8

24 pork cocktail sausages

2 tbsp mild mustard

24 ready-to-eat prunes

12 rashers smoked bacon

1 Preheat the grill. Using a sharp knife, cut a slit along the length of each sausage about three-quarters of the way through. Spread the mustard inside the slits and press a prune into each sausage.

2 Stretch the bacon with the back of a knife until each rasher is quite thin. Cut each rasher in half and wrap half a rasher of bacon around each sausage.

3 Place the sausages on a grill rack and cook under the grill, turning occasionally, for 15–20 minutes until cooked through and browned all over. Serve immediately.

sage, onion & apple stuffing

SERVES 10

550 g/1 lb 4 oz pork sausage meat

1 onion, grated

350 g/12 oz cooking apple, peeled, cored and finely chopped

25 g/1 oz fresh white breadcrumbs

2 tbsp chopped fresh sage or marjoram

grated rind of 1 lemon

1 egg, beaten

vegetable oil, for oiling

salt and pepper

sage sprig, to garnish

1 Preheat the oven to 190°C/375°F/Gas Mark 5. Place the sausage meat, onion, apple, breadcrumbs, sage, lemon rind and egg in a large bowl. Season to taste with salt and pepper and mix together until thoroughly combined.

2 Form the stuffing into balls, place on an oiled baking sheet and bake in the preheated oven for 25 minutes. Garnish with a sprig of sage and serve immediately.

3 Alternatively, place the stuffing mixture in a 900 g/2 lb loaf tin, level the surface and bake in the preheated oven for 50 minutes.

4 It is safer and more reliable to cook the stuffing separately, but if you prefer to stuff a turkey or goose, fill the neck cavity only (not the body cavity) to ensure the bird cooks all the way through. To calculate the cooking time correctly, weigh the bird after it has been stuffed.

pork, cranberry & herb stuffing

SERVES 6

1 tbsp vegetable oil, plus extra for oiling

1 onion, finely chopped

2 celery sticks, chopped

450 g/1 lb pork sausage meat

50 g/1¾ oz fresh white or wholemeal breadcrumbs

50 g/1¾ oz dried cranberries

70 g/2½ oz fresh cranberries

1 tbsp chopped fresh parsley

1 tbsp chopped fresh sage

1 tbsp chopped fresh thyme

1 large egg, beaten

salt and pepper

1 Heat the oil in a heavy-based frying pan over a medium heat, add the onion and celery and cook, stirring frequently, for 10 minutes until the onion is transparent and soft.

2 Meanwhile, preheat the oven to 190°C/375°F/Gas Mark 5. Break up the sausage meat in a large bowl. Add the breadcrumbs, dried and fresh cranberries and the herbs and mix together well. Add the cooked onion and celery, then the egg. Season well with salt and pepper and mix together thoroughly.

3 Form the stuffing into balls, place on an oiled baking sheet and bake in the preheated oven for 25 minutes. Alternatively, place the stuffing mixture in a 900 g/2 lb loaf tin, level the surface and bake in the preheated oven for 50 minutes.

4 It is safer and more reliable to cook the stuffing separately, but if you prefer to stuff a turkey or goose, fill the neck cavity only (not the body cavity) to ensure the bird cooks all the way through. To calculate the cooking time correctly, weigh the bird after it has been stuffed.

chestnut & sausage stuffing

SERVES 6–8

225 g/8 oz pork sausage meat

225 g/8 oz unsweetened chestnut purée

85 g/3 oz walnuts, chopped

115 g/4 oz ready-to-eat dried apricots, chopped

2 tbsp chopped fresh parsley

2 tbsp snipped fresh chives

2 tsp chopped fresh sage

4–5 tbsp double cream

vegetable oil, for oiling

salt and pepper

1 Preheat the oven to 190°C/375°F/Gas Mark 5. Combine the sausage meat and chestnut purée in a bowl, then stir in the walnuts, apricots, parsley, chives and sage. Stir in enough cream to make a firm, but not dry, mixture. Season to taste with salt and pepper.

2 Form the stuffing into balls, place on an oiled baking sheet and bake in the preheated oven for 25 minutes. Serve immediately.

3 Alternatively, place the stuffing mixture in a 900 g/2 lb loaf tin, level the surface and bake in the preheated oven for 50 minutes.

4 It is safer and more reliable to cook the stuffing separately, but if you prefer to stuff a turkey or goose, fill the neck cavity only (not the body cavity) to ensure the bird cooks all the way through. To calculate the cooking time correctly, weigh the bird after it has been stuffed.

festive jewelled rice

250 g/9 oz basmati rice

70 g/2½ oz red or wild rice

70 g/2½ oz ready-to-eat dried apricots

25 g/1 oz almonds, blanched

25 g/1 oz hazelnuts, toasted

1 fresh red chilli, deseeded and finely chopped

seeds of 1 pomegranate

1 tbsp finely chopped fresh parsley

1 tbsp finely chopped fresh mint

1 tbsp finely snipped fresh chives

2 tbsp white wine vinegar

6 tbsp extra virgin olive oil

1 shallot, finely chopped

salt and pepper

1 Cook the two types of rice separately according to the packet instructions. Drain and leave to cool, then tip into a large bowl.

2 Chop the apricots and nuts and add to the rice with the chilli, pomegranate seeds and the herbs. Mix together well.

3 Just before you are ready to serve, whisk the vinegar, oil and shallot together in a jug and season well with salt and pepper. Pour the dressing over the rice and mix well. Pile into a serving dish.

christmas onion gravy

SERVES 8

2 tbsp sunflower oil

450 g/1 lb onions, thinly sliced

2 garlic cloves, crushed

1 tbsp sugar

25 g/1 oz plain flour

150 ml/5 fl oz red wine

600 ml/1 pint beef or vegetable stock

2 tsp Dijon mustard

⅛ tsp gravy browning (optional)

salt and pepper

1 Heat the oil in a large, heavy-based saucepan. Add the onions, garlic and sugar and fry over a low heat for 30 minutes, stirring occasionally, until very soft and light golden.

2 Stir in the flour and cook for 1 minute. Add the red wine and bring to the boil, then simmer and beat until the mixture is smooth. Add 150 ml/5 fl oz of the stock and return the mixture to the boil. Simmer and beat again to mix thoroughly.

3 Stir in the remaining stock, Dijon mustard and gravy browning, if using. Return the mixture to the boil once more and season to taste with salt and pepper. Simmer for 20 minutes and serve hot.

bread sauce

SERVES 12

1 onion, peeled but left whole

12 cloves

1 bay leaf, plus extra leaf to garnish

6 peppercorns

600 ml/1 pint milk

115 g/4 oz fresh white breadcrumbs

25 g/1 oz butter

½ tsp freshly grated nutmeg

2 tbsp double cream (optional)

salt and pepper

1 Make 12 small holes in the onion using a skewer and stick a clove in each hole.

2 Place the onion, one bay leaf and peppercorns in a small saucepan and pour in the milk. Place over a medium heat, bring to the boil, remove from the heat, then cover and leave to infuse for 1 hour.

3 Strain the milk and discard the onion, bay leaf and peppercorns.

4 Return the milk to the rinsed-out saucepan and add the breadcrumbs. Cook the sauce over a very gentle heat until the breadcrumbs have swollen and the sauce is thick. Beat in the butter and season well with salt and pepper.

5 When ready to serve, reheat the sauce briefly, if necessary. Add the nutmeg and stir in the double cream, if using. Pour into a warmed serving bowl and serve with the turkey.

cranberry sauce

SERVES 8

**thinly pared rind and juice
of 1 lemon**

**thinly pared rind and juice
of 1 orange**

**350 g/12 oz cranberries,
thawed if frozen**

140 g/5 oz caster sugar

**2 tbsp arrowroot, mixed
with 3 tbsp cold water**

1 Cut the strips of lemon and orange rind into thin shreds and place in a heavy-based saucepan. If using fresh cranberries, rinse well and remove any stalks. Add the berries, citrus juice and sugar to the saucepan and cook over a medium heat, stirring occasionally, for 5 minutes, or until the berries begin to burst.

2 Strain the juice into a clean saucepan and reserve the cranberries. Stir the arrowroot mixture into the juice, then bring to the boil, stirring constantly, until the sauce is smooth and thickened. Remove from the heat and stir in the reserved cranberries.

3 Transfer the cranberry sauce to a bowl and leave to cool, then cover with clingfilm and chill in the refrigerator.

piccalilli

MAKES 4 X 440 G/
15½ OZ JARS

**500 g/1 lb 2 oz cauliflower,
broken into small florets**

**300 g/10½ oz deseeded
marrow or courgette,
cut into 1–2-cm/
½–¾-inch chunks**

**200 g/7 oz shallots,
cut into 1–2-cm/
½–¾-inch chunks**

**2 large dessert apples,
cored and cut into
1–2-cm/½–¾-inch chunks**

1.2 litres/2 pints cold water

55 g/2 oz salt

**850ml/1½ pints distilled
vinegar**

**5-cm/2-inch piece fresh
ginger, finely grated**

**150 g/5½ oz golden caster
sugar**

4 tbsp cornflour

3 tbsp English mustard

1½ tsp ground turmeric

1 Place the cauliflower, marrow, shallots, apples, water and salt in a large bowl and stir well. Cover the surface with greaseproof paper or clingfilm and leave to stand for 24 hours. The next day, drain, rinse well and drain again.

2 Reserve 5 tablespoons of the vinegar. Pour the remaining vinegar into a large saucepan, then add the vegetables, apples, ginger and sugar. Bring to the boil and simmer for 8–10 minutes, until the vegetables are tender but still retain some bite. Drain well, reserving the vinegar. Set the vegetables aside.

3 Mix together the cornflour, mustard, turmeric and reserved vinegar in a bowl, then pour in the hot vinegar, whisking continuously. Return to the pan. Bring to the boil, stirring until the sauce thickens. Simmer for 3–4 minutes.

4 Stir the vegetables into the sauce and remove from the heat. Spoon into warm sterilized jars and seal. If using metal lids, cover the surface with wax discs before sealing. Once cool, use straight away or store in a cool place for up to 2 months. Refrigerate after opening.

apple & date chutney

*MAKES ONE
300 G/10½ OZ JAR*

175 ml/6 fl oz cider vinegar

1 shallot, finely chopped

1 cooking apple, peeled, cored and chopped

¼ tsp ground allspice

300 g/10½ oz Medjool dates, stoned and chopped

5 tbsp honey

1 Put the vinegar, shallot, apple and allspice in a saucepan and bring to the boil. Reduce the heat and simmer for 5–8 minutes. Add the dates and honey and cook for 8–10 minutes until the dates are soft and the liquid is syrupy.

2 Remove from the heat and leave to cool. Serve straight away or pack into sterilized jars and store in the refrigerator.

pickled apricots with star anise

MAKES TWO
500 G/1 LB 2 OZ JARS

500 ml/18 fl oz cider vinegar

500 g/1 lb 2 oz unrefined caster sugar

500 g/1 lb 2 oz ready-to-eat dried apricots

2 dried chillies

4 star anise

1 Heat the vinegar and sugar in a saucepan over a medium heat, stirring until all the sugar has dissolved. Add the apricots, chillies and star anise to the saucepan and bring to the boil. Reduce the heat and simmer for 15 minutes until the syrup has thickened.

2 Ladle the apricots into sterilized jars and cover with the syrup. Leave to cool, then seal the jars and store in a dark, cool place for up to 2 weeks.

pepper & chilli jelly

MAKES ABOUT
675 G/1 LB 8 OZ

3–5 serrano red chillies, or according to taste

8 red peppers, deseeded and roughly chopped

2 Bramley apples, washed and roughly chopped

150 ml/5 fl oz white wine vinegar

1.4 litres/2½ pints water

1 tbsp coriander seeds, lightly crushed

5-cm/2-inch piece fresh ginger, peeled and grated

about 900 g/2 lb preserving sugar (see method)

225 ml/8 fl oz liquid pectin

1 Cut 2–3 chillies in half, discard the seeds and chop the flesh. Place the chillies, peppers and apples in a preserving pan with the vinegar, water, coriander seeds and ginger. Bring to the boil, then reduce the heat and simmer for 1 hour, or until the peppers are very tender. Strain through a jelly bag.

2 Once all the liquid has been extracted, measure and return to the rinsed-out preserving pan. Add the sugar, allowing 450 g/1 lb of sugar for every 600 ml/1 pint of pepper juice. Discard the seeds from 1–2 of the remaining chillies, chop the flesh and reserve. (The other chilli could be used if a very hot jelly is preferred.) Heat gently, stirring frequently, until the sugar has completely dissolved, then bring to the boil and boil rapidly for 3 minutes.

3 Leave to cool for 5 minutes. Skim, then stir in the pectin and the reserved chopped chillies. Pot into warmed sterilized jars and cover the tops with waxed discs. When completely cold, cover with cellophane or lids, label and store in a cool place.

tomato chutney

MAKES ABOUT
3.5 KG/7 LB 10 OZ

**1.5 kg/3 lb 5 oz firm ripe
tomatoes, chopped**

**450 g/1 lb Bramley apples,
peeled, cored and
chopped**

**450 g/1 lb red onions,
chopped**

**1 head of celery, chopped,
leaves discarded**

**1 green jalapeño chilli,
deseeded and chopped**

**675 g/1 lb 8 oz demerara
sugar**

**1 tsp coriander seeds,
lightly crushed**

150 ml/5 fl oz water

600 ml/1 pint malt vinegar

4 tbsp balsamic vinegar

300 g/10½ oz sultanas

1 Place the tomatoes, apples, onions, celery, chilli and sugar in a preserving pan. Tie the coriander seeds in a small piece of muslin then add to the pan together with the water and cook over a gentle heat, stirring occasionally, for 30 minutes, or until the tomatoes and apples have collapsed.

2 Add both vinegars and the sultanas and bring to the boil, then reduce the heat and simmer for 35–45 minutes, or until a thick consistency is reached.

3 Leave to cool slightly, discard the coriander seeds then pot into warmed sterilized jars. Cover with non-metallic lids, label and store in a cool place.

VARIATION

Green tomatoes can be used in this recipe, if preferred. Replace the coriander seeds with a 2.5-cm/1-inch piece of fresh ginger, peeled and grated. Add to the mixture with the tomatoes and apples.

Desserts & Treats

dark chocolate yule log

SERVES 8

butter, for greasing

150 g/5½ oz caster sugar, plus extra for sprinkling

4 eggs, separated

1 tsp almond extract

115 g/4 oz self-raising flour, plus extra for dusting

280 g/10 oz plain chocolate, broken into squares

225 ml/8 fl oz double cream

2 tbsp rum

holly, to decorate

icing sugar, for dusting

1 Preheat the oven to 190°C/375°F/Gas Mark 5. Grease with butter and line a 40 x 28-cm/16 x 11-inch Swiss roll tin, then dust with flour.

2 Reserve 2 tablespoons of the caster sugar and whisk the remainder with the egg yolks in a bowl until thick and pale. Stir in the almond extract. Whisk the egg whites in a separate grease-free bowl until soft peaks form. Gradually whisk in the reserved sugar until stiff and glossy. Sift half the flour over the egg yolk mixture and fold in, then fold in one quarter of the egg whites. Sift and fold in the remaining flour, followed by the remaining egg whites. Spoon the mixture into the tin, spreading it out evenly with a palette knife. Bake in the preheated oven for 15 minutes, until lightly golden.

3 Sprinkle caster sugar over a sheet of greaseproof paper and turn out the cake on to the paper. Roll up and leave to cool.

4 Place the chocolate in a heatproof bowl. Bring the cream to boiling point in a small saucepan, then pour it over the chocolate and stir until the chocolate has melted. Beat with an electric mixer until smooth and thick. Reserve about one third of the chocolate mixture and stir the rum into the remainder. Unroll the cake and spread the chocolate and rum mixture over. Re-roll and place on a plate or silver board. Spread the reserved chocolate mixture evenly over the top and sides. Mark with a fork so that the surface resembles tree bark. Just before serving, decorate with holly and dust with icing sugar to resemble snow.

christmas cake

MAKES ONE
20-CM/8-INCH CAKE

150 g/5½ oz raisins

**125 g/4½ oz stoned dried
dates, chopped**

125 g/4½ oz sultanas

**100 g/3½ oz glacé cherries,
rinsed**

150 ml/5 fl oz brandy

**225 g/8 oz butter,
plus extra for greasing**

200 g/7 oz caster sugar

4 eggs

grated rind of 1 orange

grated rind of 1 lemon

1 tbsp black treacle

225 g/8 oz plain flour

½ tsp salt

½ tsp baking powder

1 tsp mixed spice

**25 g/1 oz toasted almonds,
chopped**

**25 g/1 oz toasted hazelnuts,
chopped**

750 g/1 lb 10 oz marzipan

3 tbsp apricot jam, warmed

3 egg whites

650 g/1 lb 7 oz icing sugar

silver dragées, to decorate

1 Make this cake at least 3 weeks in advance. Put all the fruit in a bowl and pour over the brandy. Cover and leave to soak overnight.

2 Preheat the oven to 110°C/225°F/Gas Mark ¼. Grease a 20-cm/8-inch cake tin with butter and line it with greaseproof paper. Cream the remaining butter and the sugar in a bowl until fluffy. Gradually beat in the eggs. Stir in the citrus rind and treacle. Sift the flour, salt, baking powder and mixed spice into a separate bowl, then fold into the egg mixture. Fold in the soaked fruit and brandy and the nuts, then spoon the mixture into the cake tin.

3 Bake in the preheated oven for at least 3 hours. If it browns too quickly, cover with foil. The cake is cooked when a skewer inserted into the centre comes out clean. Remove from the oven and leave to cool on a wire rack. Store in an airtight container until required.

4 Roll out the marzipan and cut to shape to cover the top and sides of the cake. Brush the cake with the jam and press the marzipan on to the surface. Make the icing by placing the egg whites in a bowl and adding the icing sugar a little at a time, beating well until the icing is very thick and will stand up in peaks. Spread over the covered cake, using a fork to give texture. Decorate as you wish with silver dragées.

rich christmas pudding

SERVES 10–12

200 g/7 oz currants

200 g/7 oz raisins

200 g/7 oz sultanas

150 ml/5 fl oz sweet sherry

175 g/6 oz butter, plus extra for greasing

175 g/6 oz brown sugar

4 eggs, beaten

150 g/5½ oz self-raising flour

100 g/3½ oz fresh white or wholemeal breadcrumbs

50 g/1¾ oz blanched almonds, chopped

juice of 1 orange

grated rind of ½ orange

grated rind of ½ lemon

½ tsp mixed spice

holly, to decorate

icing sugar, for dusting

1 Put the currants, raisins and sultanas in a glass bowl and pour the sherry over. Cover and leave to soak for at least 2 hours.

2 Beat together the butter and brown sugar in a bowl. Beat in the eggs, then fold in the flour. Stir in the soaked fruit and the sherry with the breadcrumbs, almonds, orange juice and rind, lemon rind and mixed spice. Grease a 1.2-litre/2-pint pudding basin and spoon the mixture into it, packing it down well and leaving a gap of 2.5 cm/1 inch at the top. Cut a round of greaseproof paper 3 cm/1½ inches larger than the top of the basin, grease with butter and place over the pudding. Secure with string, then top with 2 layers of foil. Place the pudding in a saucepan filled with boiling water that reaches two-thirds of the way up the basin. Reduce the heat and simmer for 6 hours, topping up the water in the saucepan when necessary.

3 Remove from the heat and leave to cool. Renew the greaseproof paper and foil and store in the refrigerator for 2–8 weeks. To reheat, steam as before for 2 hours. Decorate with holly and a dusting of icing sugar.

traditional brandy butter

SERVES 6–8

115 g/4 oz unsalted butter, at room temperature

55 g/2 oz caster sugar

55 g/2 oz icing sugar, sifted

3 tbsp brandy

1 Cream the butter in a bowl until it is very smooth and soft. Gradually beat in both types of sugar. Add the brandy, a little at a time, beating well after each addition and taking care not to let the mixture curdle.

2 Spoon the brandy butter into a serving dish, cover and chill in the refrigerator until firm. Keep chilled until ready to serve.

christmas frosted ginger cake

SERVES 6–8

175 g/6 oz unsalted butter, softened, plus extra for greasing

175 g/6 oz unrefined caster sugar

3 large eggs, beaten

1 tbsp black treacle

2 tbsp ginger syrup

225 g/8 oz self-raising flour

1 tsp ground ginger

1 tsp ground mixed spice

1 tbsp ground almonds

2 tbsp milk

70 g/2½ oz stem ginger, chopped

edible gold or silver dragees, to decorate

icing

225 g/8 oz icing sugar

1 tsp ginger syrup

1 Preheat the oven to 160°C/325°F/Gas Mark 3. Grease a 15 x 25-cm/6 x 10-inch square cake tin and line with greaseproof paper.

2 Cream the butter and caster sugar in a large bowl until pale and fluffy. Put the eggs and treacle into a jug with the ginger syrup and whisk together. Sift the flour and spices on to a plate. Alternately add a little of the egg mixture and then a spoonful of the flour mixture to the butter and sugar mixture until you have used up both. Add the almonds and milk and mix together until you have a smooth mixture. Fold in the stem ginger pieces.

3 Spoon the cake mixture into the prepared tin, smooth the surface with a palette knife and bake in the preheated oven for 45–50 minutes until well risen and firm to the touch. Leave to cool in the tin for 10 minutes, then turn out on to a wire rack to cool completely. Remove the greaseproof paper.

4 To make the icing, put the icing sugar in a large bowl. Beat in the ginger syrup and just enough cold water to make a thick icing – be careful not to add too much water too quickly. Spread the icing over the top of the cake, letting it run down the sides. Decorate with edible gold or silver dragees.

festive mince pies

MAKES 16

200 g/7 oz plain flour, plus extra for dusting

100 g/3½ oz butter, plus extra for greasing

25 g/1 oz icing sugar

1 egg yolk

2–3 tbsp milk, plus extra for glazing

300 g/10½ oz mincemeat

icing sugar, for dusting

1 Preheat the oven to 180°C/350°F/Gas Mark 4. Grease a 16-hole tartlet tin with butter. Sift the flour into a bowl. Using your fingertips, rub in the remaining butter until the mixture resembles breadcrumbs. Stir in the sugar and egg yolk. Stir in enough milk to make a soft dough, turn out on to a lightly floured work surface and knead lightly until smooth.

2 Shape the dough into a ball and roll out to a thickness of 1 cm/½ inch. Use fluted cutters to cut out 16 rounds measuring 7 cm/2¾ inches in diameter and use to line the holes in the tartlet tin. Half-fill each pie with mincemeat. Cut out 16 star shapes from the leftover dough, brush with milk and place on top of each pie. Glaze the surface with more milk and bake in the preheated oven for 15 minutes until the pastry is a pale golden colour. Remove from the oven and leave to cool on a wire rack. Dust with icing sugar before serving.

traditional apple pie

SERVES 8

pastry

350 g/12 oz plain flour

pinch of salt

85 g/3 oz butter or margarine, chilled and diced

85 g/3 oz lard or white vegetable fat, chilled and diced

about 6 tbsp cold water

beaten egg or milk, for glazing

filling

750 g–1 kg/1 lb 10 oz– 2 lb 4 oz cooking apples, peeled, cored and sliced

125 g/4½ oz soft light brown sugar or caster sugar, plus extra for sprinkling

½–1 tsp ground cinnamon, mixed spice or ground ginger

1–2 tbsp water (optional)

1 To make the pastry, sift the flour and salt into a bowl. Add the butter and lard and rub in with the fingertips until the mixture resembles fine breadcrumbs. Add the water and gather the mixture together into a dough. Wrap the dough in clingfilm and chill in the refrigerator for 30 minutes.

2 Preheat the oven to 220°C/425°F/Gas Mark 7. Roll out almost two-thirds of the pastry thinly and use to line a deep 23-cm/9-inch pie plate or pie tin.

3 To make the filling, mix the apples with the sugar and spice and pack into the pastry case; the filling can come up above the rim. Add the water if needed, particularly if the apples are not very juicy.

4 Roll out the remaining pastry to form a lid. Dampen the edges of the pie rim with water and position the lid, pressing the edges firmly together. Trim and crimp the edges. Use the trimmings to cut out leaves or other shapes to decorate the top of the pie, dampen with water and attach. Glaze the top of the pie with beaten egg or milk, make 1–2 slits in the top and place the pie on a baking sheet.

5 Bake in the preheated oven for 20 minutes, then reduce the temperature to 180°C/350°F/Gas Mark 4 and bake for a further 30 minutes, or until the pastry is a light golden brown. Serve hot or cold, sprinkled with sugar.

festive sherry trifle

SERVES 4–6

100 g/3½ oz trifle sponges

raspberry jam, for spreading

150 ml/5 fl oz sherry

150 g/5½ oz frozen raspberries, thawed

350 g/12 oz fresh strawberries, sliced

custard

6 egg yolks

50 g/1¾ oz caster sugar

500 ml/18 fl oz milk

1 tsp vanilla extract

topping

300 ml/10 fl oz double cream

1–2 tbsp caster sugar

1 chocolate bar, crumbled

1 Spread the trifle sponges with jam, cut them into bite-sized cubes and arrange in the bottom of a large glass serving bowl. Pour over the sherry and leave to stand for 30 minutes.

2 Combine the raspberries and strawberries and spoon them over the sponges in the bowl.

3 To make the custard, put the egg yolks and sugar into a bowl and whisk together. Pour the milk into a saucepan and warm gently over a low heat. Remove from the heat and gradually stir into the egg mixture, then return the mixture to the saucepan and stir constantly over a low heat until thickened. Do not boil. Remove from the heat, pour into a bowl and stir in the vanilla. Leave to cool for 1 hour. Spread the custard over the trifle, cover with clingfilm and chill in the refrigerator for 2 hours.

4 To make the topping, whip the cream in a bowl and stir in the sugar to taste. Spread the cream over the trifle, and then scatter over the chocolate pieces. Chill in the refrigerator for 30 minutes before serving.

orange ice cream with almond praline

SERVES 6

rind of 1 large orange, with a little pith left on

100 g/3½ oz granulated sugar

100 ml/3½ fl oz water

½ tsp orange flower water

praline

225 g/8 oz unrefined caster sugar

75 ml/2½ fl oz water

125 g/4½ oz flaked almonds, toasted

butter, for greasing

ice cream

1 vanilla pod

300 ml/10 fl oz single cream

4 large egg yolks

2 tsp custard powder

50 g/1¾ oz unrefined caster sugar

300 ml/10 fl oz crème fraîche

1 Cut the orange rind into 5-cm/2-inch pieces. Put the granulated sugar and the water in a saucepan and heat gently, stirring, until the sugar has dissolved. Bring to the boil and add the orange flower water and orange rind. Reduce the heat and simmer gently for 15–20 minutes. Leave the rind to cool slightly in the syrup, then lift out, cool completely and roughly chop.

2 To make the praline, put the caster sugar and water in a saucepan and heat gently, stirring, until the sugar has dissolved. Bring to a simmer, swirling the pan, and cook until the syrup reaches a caramel-orange colour. Remove from the heat and stir in the almonds. Pour on to a sheet of greased foil, spread out and, when hard, break into shards.

3 To make the ice cream, scrape the seeds out of the vanilla pod. Put the pod and cream in a saucepan and heat gently. Put the seeds, egg yolks, custard powder and sugar in a heatproof bowl and whisk until smooth. When the cream is about to boil, remove the vanilla pod and, whisking constantly, pour the cream over the egg yolk mixture. Still stirring, pour the mixture into the pan and bring to the boil. Reduce the heat and simmer until thickened. Plunge the pan's base into a bowl of iced water, then stir until cool. Fold in the crème fraîche and orange peel. When cold, pour into a freezerproof container, cover and freeze for 12 hours. Remove from the freezer and beat to break down any ice crystals. Re-freeze and beat again, then re-freeze until solid. Serve with the praline.

cheesecake with caramel pecan nuts

SERVES 6–8

base

50 g/1¾ oz pecan nuts

150 g/5½ oz digestive biscuits, broken into pieces

50 g/1¾ oz salted butter, melted

filling

400 g/14 oz cream cheese

200 g/7 oz curd cheese

125 g/4½ oz unrefined caster sugar

3 large eggs

3 large egg yolks

200 ml/7 fl oz double cream

topping

butter, for greasing

225 g/8 oz unrefined caster sugar

5 tbsp water

70 g/2½ oz pecan nuts

1 Preheat the oven to 160°C/325°F/Gas Mark 3. To make the base, put the pecan nuts in a food processor and process briefly, then add the broken biscuits and pulse again to form crumbs. Tip into a bowl and stir in the melted butter until well combined. Press this into the base of a 20-cm/8-inch springform cake tin. Bake in the preheated oven for 10 minutes. Leave to cool.

2 To make the filling, beat the cream cheese, curd cheese and sugar together in a large bowl. Beat in the eggs and egg yolks, one at a time, until smooth. Finally, stir in the cream. Spoon over the prepared base. Bake in the preheated oven for 1 hour, then test – the cheesecake should be cooked but with a slight 'wobble' in the centre. Return to the oven for a further 10 minutes if necessary. Leave to cool in the tin.

3 To make the topping, grease a piece of foil with butter and lay it flat. Put the sugar and water in a saucepan and heat gently, stirring, until the sugar has dissolved. Bring to a simmer, swirling the saucepan rather than stirring, and cook until the syrup begins to darken to form the caramel, then add the pecan nuts. Lift each pecan nut out on to the greased foil and leave to harden. When you are ready to serve, unmould the cheesecake on to a serving plate and arrange the caramel pecan nuts on top.

chocolate chestnut roulade

SERVES 6

6 large eggs, separated

150 g/5½ oz unrefined caster sugar

½ tsp vanilla or chocolate extract

50 g/1¾ oz cocoa powder

icing sugar, for dusting

250 ml/9 fl oz double cream

250 g/9 oz sweetened chestnut purée

2 tbsp brandy

70 g/2½ oz cooked peeled chestnuts, chopped

1 Preheat the oven to 180°C/350°F/Gas Mark 4. Line a 23 x 45-cm/9 x 17¾-inch Swiss roll tin with baking paper.

2 Using an electric whisk, beat the egg yolks, caster sugar and vanilla extract together in a bowl for 10 minutes, or until doubled in volume and pale and fluffy. In a separate clean bowl, whisk the egg whites until they form soft peaks. Fold a tablespoonful of egg whites into the egg yolk mixture, then gently fold in the remaining egg whites and the cocoa powder.

3 Spoon the cake mixture into the prepared tin and smooth the surface with a palette knife. Bake in the preheated oven for 20 minutes until risen. Leave to cool in the tin.

4 Put a large piece of baking paper over a clean tea towel and dust with icing sugar, invert the sponge on to the baking paper and carefully peel away the lining paper. In a clean bowl, whisk the cream until stiff, then stir in the chestnut purée and the brandy. Spread over the sponge, leaving a 2.5-cm/1-inch margin around the edges, and scatter over the chestnuts. Using one end of the tea towel, carefully roll up the roulade. Dust with more icing sugar to serve.

roast plums with armagnac fool

SERVES 6

24 ripe plums

50 g/1¾ oz unsalted butter, plus extra for greasing

2 tbsp maple syrup or flower honey

300 ml/10 fl oz double cream

2 tbsp icing sugar

2 large egg whites

2 tbsp Armagnac or brandy

finely grated rind of 1 lemon

1 tsp rosewater (optional)

1 Preheat the oven to 200°C/400°F/Gas Mark 6. Grease a baking dish with butter.

2 Cut each plum in half and remove and discard the stone. Place cut-sides up on the prepared baking dish, dot each plum with some of the butter and drizzle over the maple syrup. Cover with foil. Bake in the preheated oven for 20–25 minutes until tender. Leave to cool.

3 Whisk the cream in a bowl until beginning to thicken, adding the sugar a little at a time. In a separate bowl, whisk the egg whites until stiff. Stir the Armagnac into the cream, then fold in the egg whites, followed by half the lemon rind.

4 To serve, divide the plum halves among 6 serving dishes, drizzle over the rosewater, if using. Spoon the fool on top of the plums, scatter over the remaining lemon rind and serve immediately.

christmas spiced loaf

SERVES 6

450 g/1 lb strong white flour, plus extra for dusting

pinch of salt

2 tsp mixed spice

115 g/4 oz unsalted butter, chilled and diced

7-g/⅛-oz sachet easy-blend dried yeast

115 g/4 oz unrefined caster sugar

115 g/4 oz currants

115 g/4 oz raisins

50 g/1¾ oz mixed peel, chopped

finely grated rind of 1 orange

1 egg, beaten

150 ml/5 fl oz milk, warmed

vegetable oil, for oiling

1 Sift the flour, salt and mixed spice into a bowl and rub in the butter until the mixture resembles breadcrumbs. Stir in the yeast, sugar, dried fruit, mixed peel and orange rind, then add the egg and the warm milk and bring together to form a soft dough. Knead the dough briefly on a floured work surface. Flour a clean bowl and add the dough. Cover the bowl and leave to rise in a warm place for 2 hours.

2 Preheat the oven to 180°C/350°F/Gas Mark 4 and oil a 900-g/2-lb loaf tin. Knead the dough again briefly, then place it in the tin, cover and leave to prove for 20 minutes. Bake in the preheated oven for 1 hour 10 minutes – the loaf should be golden and well risen. Leave to cool in the tin.

cranberry muffins

MAKES 18

225 g/8 oz plain flour

2 tsp baking powder

½ tsp salt

50 g/1¾ oz caster sugar

55 g/2 oz unsalted butter, melted, plus extra for greasing

2 eggs, lightly beaten

175 ml/6 fl oz milk

115 g/4 oz fresh cranberries

50 g/1¾ oz Parmesan cheese, freshly grated

1 Preheat the oven to 200°C/400°F/Gas Mark 6. Lightly grease two 9-cup muffin tins with butter.

2 Sift the flour, baking powder and salt into a bowl. Stir in the sugar. Combine the melted butter, eggs and milk in a separate bowl, then pour into the bowl of dry ingredients. Stir until all of the ingredients are evenly combined, then stir in the fresh cranberries.

3 Divide the mixture evenly between the prepared 18 cups in the muffin tins. Sprinkle the grated Parmesan cheese over the top. Bake in the preheated oven for 20 minutes until risen and golden.

4 Remove the muffins from the oven and leave to cool slightly in the tins. Transfer the muffins on to a wire rack and leave to cool completely.

christmas bells

MAKES ABOUT 30

225 g/8 oz butter, softened

140 g/5 oz caster sugar

finely grated rind of 1 lemon

1 egg yolk, lightly beaten

280 g/10 oz plain flour

½ tsp ground cinnamon

salt

100 g/3½ oz plain chocolate chips

30 silver balls and food colouring pens, to decorate

icing

2 tbsp lightly beaten egg white

2 tbsp lemon juice

225 g/8 oz icing sugar

1 Put the butter, sugar and lemon rind into a bowl and mix well with a wooden spoon, then beat in the egg yolk. Sift the flour, cinnamon and a pinch of salt into the mixture, add the chocolate chips and stir until thoroughly combined. Halve the dough, shape into balls, wrap in clingfilm and chill in the refrigerator for 30–60 minutes.

2 Preheat the oven to 190°C/375°F/Gas Mark 5. Line 2 baking sheets with baking parchment. Unwrap the dough and roll out between 2 sheets of baking parchment. Stamp out cookies with a 5-cm/2-inch bell-shaped cutter and put them on the prepared baking sheets spaced well apart.

3 Bake for 10–15 minutes, until light golden brown. Leave to cool on the baking sheets for 5–10 minutes, then using a palette knife, carefully transfer to wire racks to cool completely.

4 To make the icing, mix together the egg white and lemon juice in a bowl, then gradually beat in the icing sugar until smooth. Leave the cookies on the racks and spread the icing over them. Place a silver ball on the clapper shape at the bottom of each cookie and leave to set completely. When the icing is dry, use the food colouring pens to draw patterns on the cookies.

christmas tree biscuits

MAKES 12

150 g/5½ oz plain flour, plus extra for dusting

1 tsp ground cinnamon

½ tsp freshly grated nutmeg

½ tsp ground ginger

70 g/2½ oz unsalted butter, diced, plus extra for greasing

3 tbsp honey

white icing and silver dragées (optional) and narrow ribbon, to decorate

1 Sift the flour and spices into a bowl and rub in the butter until the mixture resembles breadcrumbs. Add the honey and mix together well to form a soft dough. Halve the dough, shape into balls, wrap in clingfilm and chill in the refrigerator for 30 minutes.

2 Preheat the oven to 180°C/350°F/Gas Mark 4 and lightly grease 2 baking sheets with butter. Roll out one piece of dough on a floured work surface to about 5 mm/¼ inch thick. Cut out tree shapes using a cutter or cardboard template. Repeat with the remaining dough.

3 Put the biscuits on the prepared baking sheets and, using a cocktail stick, make a hole through the top of each biscuit large enough to thread the ribbon through. Chill in the refrigerator for 15 minutes.

4 Bake in the preheated oven for 10–12 minutes until golden. Leave to cool on the baking sheets for 5 minutes, then transfer to a wire rack to cool completely. Decorate the trees with icing and silver dragées, or leave them plain. Thread the ribbon through and hang on the Christmas tree.

christmas angels

MAKES ABOUT 25

225 g/8 oz butter, softened

140 g/5 oz caster sugar

1 egg yolk, lightly beaten

2 tsp passion fruit pulp

280 g/10 oz plain flour

salt

55 g/2 oz desiccated coconut

edible silver glitter, to decorate

icing

175 g/6 oz icing sugar

1–1½ tbsp passion fruit pulp

1 Put the butter and sugar into a bowl and mix well with a wooden spoon, then beat in the egg yolk and passion fruit pulp. Sift the flour and a pinch of salt into the mixture, add the coconut and stir until thoroughly combined. Halve the dough, shape into balls, wrap in clingfilm and chill in the refrigerator for 30–60 minutes.

2 Preheat the oven to 190°C/375°F/Gas Mark 5. Line 2 baking sheets with baking parchment. Unwrap the dough and roll out between 2 sheets of baking parchment. Stamp out cookies with a 7-cm/2¾-inch angel-shaped cutter and put them on the prepared baking sheets spaced well apart.

3 Bake for 10–15 minutes, until light golden brown. Leave to cool on the baking sheets for 5–10 minutes, then using a palette knife, carefully transfer to wire racks to cool completely.

4 To make the icing, sift the icing sugar into a bowl and stir in the passion fruit pulp until the icing has the consistency of thick cream. Leave the cookies on the racks and spread the icing over them. Sprinkle with the edible glitter and leave to set.

chocolate truffle selection

MAKES 40–50

225 g/8 oz plain chocolate, minimum 70% cocoa solids

175 ml/6 fl oz whipping cream

cocoa powder, icing sugar or chopped toasted almonds, for coating

1 Roughly chop the chocolate and put in a large heatproof bowl. Put the cream in a saucepan and bring up to boiling point. Pour over the chocolate and whisk until smooth. Leave to cool at room temperature for 1½–2 hours.

2 Cover 2 baking sheets with clingfilm or baking paper. Using a teaspoon, take bite-sized scoops of the chocolate mixture and roll in cocoa powder, icing sugar or chopped nuts to form balls, then place on the prepared baking sheets and chill in the refrigerator until set.

dark & white chocolate florentines

MAKES 20

5 g/1 oz unsalted butter,
plus extra for greasing

70 g/2½ oz unrefined
caster sugar

15 g/½ oz plain flour,
plus extra for dusting

4 tbsp double cream

50 g/1¾ oz whole blanched
almonds, roughly
chopped

50 g/1¾ oz flaked almonds,
toasted

50 g/1¾ oz mixed peel,
chopped

50 g/1¾ oz undyed glacé
cherries, chopped

50 g/1¾ oz preserved stem
ginger, drained and
chopped

70 g/2½ oz plain chocolate,
minimum 70% cocoa
solids, broken into
pieces

70 g/2½ oz white chocolate,
broken into pieces

1 Preheat the oven to 190°C/375°F/Gas Mark 5. Lightly grease 2 baking sheets with butter and dust with flour, shaking to remove any excess.

2 Put the remaining butter, sugar and flour in a small saucepan and heat gently, stirring well, until the mixture has melted. Gradually add the cream, stirring constantly, then add all the remaining ingredients, except the chocolate, and stir thoroughly. Remove from the heat and leave to cool.

3 Drop 5 teaspoonfuls of the mixture on to each of the prepared baking sheets, spaced well apart to allow for spreading, then flatten with the back of a spoon. Bake in the preheated oven for 12–15 minutes. Leave the biscuits to harden on the sheets for 2–3 minutes before transferring to a wire rack. Repeat with the remaining mixture, again using the 2 baking sheets.

4 When the biscuits are completely cool, put the plain chocolate in a heatproof bowl, set the bowl over a saucepan of barely simmering water and heat until melted. Using a teaspoon, spread the base of 10 of the biscuits with the melted chocolate and place chocolate side-up on a wire rack to set. Repeat with the white chocolate and the remaining 10 biscuits.

peanut brittle

MAKES ABOUT
500 G/1 LB 2 OZ

**vegetable or sunflower oil,
for oiling**

**200 g/7 oz granulated
sugar**

**85 g/3 oz soft light brown
sugar**

85 g/3 oz golden syrup

25 g/1 oz butter

6 tbsp water

**175 g/6 oz salted peanuts,
roughly chopped**

1 tsp vanilla extract

¼ tsp bicarbonate of soda

1 Preheat the oven to 120°C/250°F/Gas Mark ½. Line a 30-cm/12-inch square baking pan with foil and oil lightly. Place in the preheated oven to warm.

2 Meanwhile, place the sugars, golden syrup, butter and water in a heavy-based saucepan. Heat gently, stirring until the butter has melted and the sugar has completely dissolved.

3 Brush around the inside of the pan above the level of the syrup with a pastry brush dipped in water, then turn up the heat and boil rapidly until the syrup reaches 150°C/300°F ('hard crack' stage).

4 Working quickly, remove from the heat and stir in the peanuts followed by the vanilla extract and bicarbonate of soda. Pour onto the warmed baking tray and tip gently to level the surface. Leave for about 30 minutes to cool, then snap into pieces. Store in airtight bags or containers.

mulled ale & mulled wine

MULLED ALE
MAKES 2.8
LITRES/5 PINTS

2.5 litres/4½ pints strong ale

300 ml/10 fl oz brandy

2 tbsp caster sugar

large pinch of ground cloves

large pinch of ground ginger

MULLED WINE
MAKES 3.3
LITRES/5½ PINTS

5 oranges

50 cloves

thinly pared rind and juice of 4 lemons

850 ml/1½ pints water

115 g/4 oz caster sugar

2 cinnamon sticks

2 litres/3½ pints red wine

150 ml/5 fl oz brandy

1 To make the mulled ale, put all the ingredients in a heavy-based saucepan and heat gently, stirring, until the sugar has dissolved. Continue to heat so that it is simmering but not boiling. Remove the saucepan from the heat and serve the ale immediately in heatproof glasses.

2 To make the mulled wine, prick the skins of 3 of the oranges all over with a fork and stud with the cloves, then set aside. Thinly pare the rind and squeeze the juice from the remaining oranges.

3 Put the orange rind and juice, lemon rind and juice, water, sugar and cinnamon in a heavy-based saucepan and bring to the boil over a medium heat, stirring occasionally, until the sugar has dissolved. Boil for 2 minutes without stirring, then remove from the heat, stir once and leave to stand for 10 minutes. Strain the liquid into a heatproof jug.

4 Pour the wine into a separate saucepan and add the strained spiced juices, the brandy and the clove-studded oranges. Simmer gently without boiling, then remove the saucepan from the heat. Strain into heatproof glasses and serve immediately.

hot rum punch

MAKES 4.3
LITRES/7½ PINTS

850 ml/1½ pints rum

850 ml/1½ pints brandy

**600 ml/1 pint freshly
squeezed lemon juice**

3–4 tbsp caster sugar

**2 litres/3½ pints boiling
water**

slices of fruit, to decorate

1 Mix together the rum, brandy, lemon juice and 3 tablespoons of the sugar in a punch bowl or large heatproof mixing bowl. Pour in the boiling water and stir well to mix. Taste and add more sugar if required. Decorate with the fruit slices and serve immediately in heatproof glasses with handles.

cinnamon apple cup

MAKES 3.7 LITRES/6½ PINTS

40 cloves

2 apples, cored, quartered and thickly sliced

2 oranges, quartered and thickly sliced

4 cinnamon sticks

1.7 litres/3 pints pressed apple juice

600 ml/1 pint orange juice

600 ml/1 pint dark rum (optional)

1 Insert one clove into each apple slice and place in a large saucepan with the orange pieces, cinnamon sticks, apple juice and orange juice.

2 Place over a low heat and simmer for 20 minutes to allow the flavours to infuse.

3 Remove the pan from the heat. Add rum, if using, and serve warm, ladled into heatproof glasses.

real hot chocolate

SERVES 1–2

40 g/1½ oz plain chocolate, broken into pieces

300 ml/10 fl oz milk

chocolate curls, to decorate

1 Place the chocolate in a large heatproof jug. Place the milk in a heavy-based saucepan and bring to the boil. Pour about one quarter of the milk onto the chocolate and leave until the chocolate has softened.

2 Whisk the milk and chocolate mixture until smooth. Return the remaining milk to the heat and return to the boil, then pour onto the chocolate mixture, whisking constantly.

3 Pour into warmed mugs or cups and decorate with chocolate curls. Serve immediately.

VARIATION

To vary the flavour, add a teaspoon of coffee essence (or strong black coffee), or heat a cinnamon stick or cardamom seed with the milk, then remove this before mixing with the chocolate. Decorate with mini marshmallows or a swirl of whipped cream and a dusting of cocoa powder.